Obama-ology
by **Aurin Squire**

M000205961

Cast in order of appearance

Instructors | **Peter Caulfield, Pearl Mackie**
Katherine Newman, Amanda Wright
Warren | **Edward Dede**
Sam | **Peter Caulfield**
Barbara | **Amanda Wright**
Resident #1 | **Amanda Wright**
Resident #2 | **Peter Caulfield**
Resident #3 | **Katherine Newman**
Cece | **Pearl Mackie**
Laura | **Katherine Newman**
Cop #1 | **Peter Caulfield**
Store Clerk | **Katherine Newman**
Cop #2 | **Peter Caulfield**
Lainey | **Katherine Newman**
Brad | **Peter Caulfield**
Caits | **Pearl Mackie**
Neighbor | **Amanda Wright**
Night Cop | **Peter Caulfield**
Mom | **Amanda Wright**
Dad | **Peter Caulfield**

The play takes place in the rental cars, street corners, and campaign offices of Cleveland, Ohio, during the 2008 US presidential election.

The performance lasts approximately two hours.
There will be one interval of fifteen minutes.

Playwright | **Aurin Squire**
Director | **Tommo Fowler**
Designer | **Anna Lewis**
Lighting Designer | **Rob Mills**
Composer and Sound Designer | **Finn Keane**
Movement Director | **Ita O'Brien**
Assistant Director | **Emerald Crankson**
Dialect Coach | **Nina Zendejas**
Casting Director | **Georgia Fleury Reynolds**
Producer | **Aidan Grounds**
Production Company | **ABG Productions**

CAST

PETER CAULFIELD
INSTRUCTOR, SAM, RESIDENT #2, COP 1,
COP 2, NIGHT COP, BRAD AND DAD

Productions at the Finborough Theatre
include *Lark Rise to Candleford*.
Theatre includes *One Man, Two Guvnors*
(West End and National Tour), *The Man
of Mode, A Funny Thing Happened On
the Way to the Forum* (National Theatre),
Enron (Chichester Festival Theatre, Royal
Court Theatre and Noël Coward Theatre),
The Wild Duck (Donmar Warehouse), *Into
the Woods* (Royal Opera House, Covent
Garden), *Aladdin* (The Old Vic) and *Nicked*
(HighTide).
Television includes *Cucumber* and *Banana*,
both airing in January 2015.

PEARL MACKIE
INSTRUCTOR, CECE, CAITS

Productions at the Finborough Theatre
include *The Rain That Does Not Make You
Wet* as part of *Vibrant 2013 – A Festival of
Finborough Playwrights*.
Trained at Bristol Old Vic Theatre School.
Theatre includes *Disnatured* (Shakespeare
in Shoreditch Festival), *Crystal Springs* (Park
Theatre), *Neighbors* (HighTide), *Brothers
in Blood, Elusive Spring* (Bilimankwhe
Arts), *Blue Blood* (Riverside Studios), *Only
Human* (Theatre503),*The Helen Project*
(Lost Theatre, Stockwell), *Beef* (Southwark
Playhouse) *Home* (The Last Refuge), *Hiding,
Losing, Survivors* (Chichester Festival
Theatre – Playpod) and *Ma Kelly Goes to the
Games* (Attic Theatre).
Film includes *Svengali*.
Television includes *Doctors*.
Radio includes *Romeo and Juliet*.

EDWARD DEDE
WARREN

Trained at the London Academy of Music
and Dramatic Art.
Theatre includes *Design For Living* (The Old
Vic), *Shoot/Get Treasure/Repeat* (Paines
Plough at the Village Underground), *Soho
Slam* (Soho Theatre), *Dr Faustus* (Watford
Palace Theatre), *Gleaming Dark – Burnt
Butterflies* (Trafalgar Studios), *Present:Tense*
(Nabokov at Trafalgar Studios), *Pirates*
(Polka Theatre), *Sinbad the Untold Tale*
(Theatre By the Lake, Keswick) and *Barren*
(The 24 Hour Plays at The Old Vic).
Film includes *Farming, 80 Days* and *Hamlet*.
Television includes *The Wrong Door* and
Shangri-La.
Radio includes *A Dangerous Voyage*.

ABG Productions in association with Neil McPherson
for the Finborough Theatre presents

The European Premiere

Obama-ology
by **Aurin Squire**

FINBOROUGH | THEATRE

First performed at the Juilliard School, New York City: Wednesday, 3 September 2014.
First performed at the Finborough Theatre: Sunday, 30 November 2014.

KATHERINE NEWMAN
INSTRUCTOR, LAURA, RESIDENT #3,
STORE CLERK AND LAINEY

Trained at Queen Margaret's University,
Edinburgh.
Theatre includes *See What I See* (Burton
Taylor Studio at Oxford Playhouse),
Where the Love Lies (Theatre503), *The
Day After* (Pleasance London), *Prophesy,
Macbeth* (BAZ), *R U L8* (Everyman Theatre,
Cheltenham) and *Much Ado About Nothing*
(Byre Theatre, St Andrews).
Film includes *Woman at the Well,
Beatitudes, Cannibals, Crossing the Line,
And the Colours Are Like Summer, Heim*
and *Once Upon A Time*.
Television includes *Locked Up Abroad*
and *Tomorrow's Child*.
Katherine also provides voice overs for
Sky, Channel 4, MTV and is the voice of
Professor McGonagall for the Harry Potter
Warner Brothers Kinect game.

Sunday (Tricycle Theatre), *How To Get
Them* (Arcola Theatre), *The Black History
Month Project* (Bush Theatre), *Big Break*
(Hampstead Theatre) and *Heart of a Dog*
(Assembly Rooms, Edinburgh).
Film includes *Here for You, All the World,
30 Seconds, Consent, Stripping the Illusion*
and *Silent Voices*.
Television includes *Euphoria, Prime
Suspect 7, Doctors, Midsomer Murders*
and *Making It at Holby*.
Amanda also voices all Disney UK audio
descriptions of *Hannah Montana*.

AMANDA WRIGHT
INSTRUCTOR, BARBARA, RESIDENT #1,
NEIGHBOR AND MOM

Productions at the Finborough Theatre
include *Achidi J's Final Hours*.
Trained at the Royal Central School of
Speech and Drama.
Theatre includes *Horrible Histories, Horrible
Science* (Birmingham Stage Company),
The 24 Hour Plays (The Old Vic), *Henry V*
(Orange Tree Theatre, Richmond), *Handa's
Surprise, Goldilocks* (Little Angel Theatre),
Called to Account (Roundhouse), *Bloody*

CREATIVE

AURIN SQUIRE
PLAYWRIGHT

Aurin Squire is a New York playwright, screenwriter, and reporter. He is a two-time recipient of the Lecomte du Nouy Prize from Lincoln Center. In 2014-2015 he has fellowships at The Dramatists Guild of America, National Black Theatre, and Brooklyn Arts Exchange. Squire is the winner of the Act One Writing Contest at Lincoln Center Theatre. His plays include *The Great Black Sambo Machine* (Lincoln Centre Lab and Ars Nova), *To Whom It May Concern* (Abingdon Theatre and ArcLight Theatre productions), and *African Americana* (Theatre503). Last year his drama *Freefalling* (Barrington Stages) won the Fiat Lux Prize from the New York Catholic Church as well as 2014 first prize in the InspiraTO Theatre International Play Festival in Toronto. As a screenwriter, he adapted the novel *Velocity* into a screenplay for indie film company, Moxie Picture. He also wrote the multimedia short film on Jewish immigrants coming to America, *Dreams of Freedom*. *Dreams* won three national museum awards and is a permanent exhibit at the National Museum of American Jewish History. Currently, Squire has a Lila Acheson Wallace American Playwrights Fellowship at The Juilliard School.

TOMMO FOWLER
DIRECTOR

Productions at the Finborough Theatre include Assistant Director of *Sommer 14: A Dance of Death*.
Trained with Living Pictures / Elen Bowman and on the Short Course at the Royal Academy of Dramatic Art.
As a Director, theatre includes *Monster Party* (Arcola Theatre), *Vesting Day* (Southwark Playhouse), *The Repast*, *Porcelain*, *Just Say No* (Theatre503), a rehearsed reading of *Wake* (English Touring Theatre Studios), *The (Accidental) Execution of Alan Bishop* (Pleasance London), *Multiple Choice* (Lost Theatre, Stockwell), *Taketh* (Take Courage Theatre, New Cross), *Extremely Brief and Violent* (Royal Academy of Dramatic Art). Assistant Direction includes *Handel Furioso* (Arcola Theatre and National Tour), *Rainbow* – winner of Fringe First Award (Edinburgh Festival) and *Mojo Mickybo* (Old Red Lion Theatre).
Dramaturgy includes *No Border*, an intranational verbatim theatre project. Tommo is also Development Associate at ABG Productions, a Reader for the Bush Theatre and Theatre503 and Project Manager for Living Pictures.

ANNA LEWIS
DESIGNER

Productions at the Finborough Theatre include *Rachel* and *The White Carnation* which transferred to the Jermyn Street Theatre.
Set Designs include *The Sorcerer* (Buxton Opera House) and *Twelfth Night* (International Tour to Japan, Bodleian Library Oxford, Southwark Playhouse and The Mill Studio, Guildford). Costume Designs include *The Nativity Goes Wrong*, *Look Back in Anger* and *Miss Julie* (Reading Rep). Set and Costume Designs include *Bound* (Pegasus Theatre, Oxford), *Middle England* (Burton Taylor Studio, Oxford), *Ghosts* (Greenwich Theatre), and *The Hothouse*, *The Picture of Dorian Grey*, *The Seagull* and *A Streetcar Named Desire* (Oxford Playhouse). Assistant Costume Designs include *The Keepers of Infinite Space* (Park Theatre), *The Hotel Plays* (Langham Hotel) and the Dorfman Opening Gala (National Theatre). Assistant Set and Costume Designs include *Ace of Clubs* (Union Theatre). Film includes Production Designer on *Round and Round the Garden*, *Mary* and *The Wishing Horse*, and Costume Designer on *The Sanctuary of Collei*, nominated for an award for achievement in costume in the Southampton Film Festival. Anna is also part of the costume team for Secret Cinema and has worked as a costume assistant on eight of their large-scale projects including *Dirty Dancing*, *Millers Crossing*, *The Grand Budapest Hotel* and *Back to the Future*.

ROB MILLS
LIGHTING DESIGNER

Productions at the Finborough Theatre include Lighting Designer for *Free as Air* and *Gay's the Word* which transferred to the Jermyn Street Theatre, and Lighting and Video Designer for *Sommer 14: A Dance of Death*.

Lighting Designs include *Crows on the Wire* (Northern Ireland Tour), *Romeo and Juliet* (Cambridge Arts Theatre), *Oedipus Retold*, *Making Dickie Happy* (Tristan Bates Theatre), *Tosca* (National Tour and Luxembourg National Cultural Centre), *Salad Days*, *The Biograph Girl*, *Daredevas* (Waterman's Theatre), *Gilbert is Dead* (Hoxton Hall), *Love Bites* (Leatherhead Theatre), *The Elixir of Love* (Stanley Hall Opera), *Napoleon Noir* (Shaw Theatre), *The Lion, the Witch and the Wardrobe*, *Hayton on Homicide* (Edinburgh Festival) and *Niceties* (Cambridge Footlights).

Production and Lighting Designs include *Aida* (Epsom Playhouse), *Madama Butterfly* (Harlequin Theatre), *Venus and Adonis*, *Dido and Aeneas*, *The Magic Flute* (Upstairs at the Gatehouse), *The Mikado*, *The Yeomen of the Guard* (Minack Theatre), *Don Giovanni*, *Pelléas et Mélisande* (West Road Concert Hall) and *Crave* (Edinburgh Fringe).

Rob has also provided the lighting and event design for a large number of live and corporate events for his company Light Motif including the 2010 'Floating Finale' to the Lord Mayor's Show on the River Thames.

www.robwmills.co.uk.

FINN KEANE
COMPOSER AND SOUND DESIGNER

Trained at the University of Oxford, specialising in composition.

As a Composer, theatre includes *Lysistrata* (Edinburgh Festival), *Angels in America* (Oxford Playhouse) and *The Glass Menagerie* (Corpus Auditorium at Corpus Christi College, Oxford).

Film includes *LICK*, *Killing Kidz*, *Three Speech* and *The Secret*, and as Sound Designer, *The Wishing Horse*, winner of Best London Film at the Portobello Road Film Festival 2014.

Television includes the forthcoming *War Art* with Eddie Redmayne.

ITA O'BRIEN
MOVEMENT DIRECTOR

Productions at the Finborough Theatre as an actor include *Stroke Me*.

Trained as an actor at Bristol Old Vic and as a Movement Director at the Royal Central School of Speech and Drama.

Theatre includes *Pillars of the Community*, *Aristocrats* (National Theatre), *King Lear* (The Old Vic), *Romeo and Juliet* (National Tour and the Hong Kong Arts Festival) and *The Three Birds* (Gate Theatre).

As a Movement Director, theatre includes *The Indian Boy* (Royal Shakespeare Company), *The Winter's Tale* (Shakespeare's Globe), *Othello* (Salisbury Playhouse), *Purcell's Dido* and *Aeneas* (Bussey Building), *OMG: Ovid Unplugged* (Square Chapel, Halifax), *The Tempest* (Ivy Arts Centre, Guildford), *The Front Room* (The Drill Hall), *The Southwark Mysteries* (Southwark Cathedral) and *Back At You* (Battersea Arts Centre).

Television includes coaching Juliet Stevenson for *Atlantis*.

Ita is also a teacher at the London Academy of Music and Dramatic Art, the Royal Central School of Speech and Drama and Drama Centre.

As a Director, Ita recently devised *April's Fool* (Westwood Theatre) and co-created *The Faun* (St Andrews Church). She is currently working on her next piece *does my sex offend you?* to be performed in 2015.

EMERALD CRANKSON
ASSISTANT DIRECTOR

Trained with The Young Vic and the National Youth Theatre.

Assistant Direction includes *The Island*, *The Web* (The Young Vic) and *And Now: The World* (Openworks Theatre).

As an Actor, theatre includes *Noughts and Crosses* (The Young Vic), *Orpheus and Eurydice*, *Relish* (National Youth Theatre) and *Somewhere in Södermalm* (Etcetera Theatre). Television includes *Youngers II* and *Brothers With No Game*.

NINA ZENDEJAS
DIALECT COACH

Trained at the Royal Central School of Speech and Drama and Boston Conservatory

Theatre in the UK includes *Twelfth Night*, *The Wind in the Willows* (Royal Central School of Speech and Drama) and *London – Let's Get Visceral* (Old Vic Theatre). Theatre in Boston, Massachusetts, includes *Translations*, *Nine* (Stranford Calderwood Pavilion), *Working*, *One Man, Two Guvnors*, *Stones in His Pockets*, *By the Way*, *Meet Vera Stark*, and *On the Town* (Lyric Stage), *The Seabirds* (Boston Playwrights Theatre), *Hedda Gabler and Rock n' Roll* (Cambridge YMCA Theatre), *Necessary Targets*, *Sweeney Todd*, *One Touch of Venus*, *Nine* (Boston Conservatory Theatre), *Rent* and *Grimm* (Boston Arts Academy Theatre).

AIDAN GROUNDS
PRODUCER

Productions at the Finborough Theatre include *Rachel* and *Armstrong's War*. Aidan founded ABG Productions in April 2013. He is a recipient of the Stage One Bursary for New Producers and is mentored by Caro Newling.
Other productions include *Jekyll and Hyde* (Southwark Playhouse).
Film includes *The Wishing Horse* with Richard E. Grant (Award of Excellence Best Shorts Competition).
Aidan is also Executive Director at Reading Repertory Theatre.

Sunday/Monday/Tuesday Productions at the Finborough Theatre

The Finborough Theatre is committed to its multi-award-winning artistic policy of presenting both plays and music theatre, concentrated exclusively on vibrant new writing and unique rediscoveries of neglected work from the 19th and 20th centuries. Our Sunday/Monday/
Tuesday productions (nine performances on Sunday and Monday evenings and Tuesday matinees, playing over a three week period, in repertoire with our main show) allow us to produce even more work that we believe deserves to be seen – often directed by exciting emerging directors. Sunday/Monday/Tuesday productions are performed on the set and with the lighting rig of our main show.

Finborough Theatre Commissions

Obama-ology is a Finborough Theatre commission. Finborough Theatre commissions are works specially chosen for the Finborough Theatre by Artistic Director Neil McPherson, and either produced in-house, or in partnership with some of the UK's most exciting producers.

Production Acknowledgements

This production is indebted to the generous support of The Richard Carne Trust.

With special thanks to

WorkSpace, Emily Precious, Alex Forsyth, Hatty Jones, Carla Kingham, Daniel Sonabend, Hannah Groombridge, Chelsea Walker, Ruth and Graham Fowler, Elen Bowman and Simon Lewis.

ABG Productions was established in May 2013 by producers Aidan Grounds and Emily Precious. It is a company dedicated to creating artistically exciting, visually impressive, technically ambitious, and financially viable theatre and film.

It aims to provide support for directors to realise their creative vision, whether this involves a large company of actors and an orchestra in a large playhouse venue or a cast of two in a small black-box studio, from concept-driven music video to narrative script-driven film.

Previous theatre productions include *Rachel* and *Armstrong's War* (Finborough Theatre) and *Jekyll and Hyde* (Southwark Playhouse).

Producers
Aidan Grounds
Emily Precious

Executive Producer
Adam Baghdadi

Development Associates
Tommo Fowler
Jack Peters

Production Associate
Rachel Beaconsfield-Press

ABG Productions are delighted to be supported by the Stage One Bursary for New Producers.

FINBOROUGH | THEATRE

VIBRANT **NEW WRITING** | UNIQUE **REDISCOVERIES**

118 Finborough Road, London SW10 9ED
admin@finboroughtheatre.co.uk | www.finboroughtheatre.co.uk

"A disproportionately valuable component of the London theatre ecology. Its programme combines new writing and revivals, in selections intelligent and audacious."
Financial Times

"The tiny but mighty Finborough… one of the best batting averages of any London company."
Ben Brantley, *The New York Times*

"The Finborough Theatre, under the artistic direction of Neil McPherson, has been earning a place on the must-visit list with its eclectic, smartly curated slate of new works and neglected masterpieces."
Vogue

Founded in 1980, the multi-award-winning Finborough Theatre presents plays and music theatre, concentrated exclusively on vibrant new writing and unique rediscoveries from the 19th and 20th centuries. Behind the scenes, we continue to discover and develop a new generation of theatre makers – through our Literary team, and our programmes for both interns and Resident Assistant Directors.

Despite remaining completely unsubsidised, the Finborough Theatre has an unparalleled track record of attracting the finest creative talent who go on to become leading voices in British theatre. Under Artistic Director Neil McPherson, it has discovered some of the UK's most exciting new playwrights including Laura Wade, James Graham, Mike Bartlett, Sarah Grochala, Jack Thorne, Simon

Vinnicombe, Alexandra Wood, Al Smith, Nicholas de Jongh and Anders Lustgarten; and directors including Blanche McIntyre.

Artists working at the theatre in the 1980s included Clive Barker, Rory Bremner, Nica Burns, Kathy Burke, Ken Campbell, Jane Horrocks and Claire Dowie. In the 1990s, the Finborough Theatre first became known for new writing including Naomi Wallace's first play *The War Boys*; Rachel Weisz in David Farr's *Neville Southall's Washbag*; four plays by Anthony Neilson including *Penetrator* and *The Censor*, both of which transferred to the Royal Court Theatre; and new plays by Richard Bean, Lucinda Coxon, David Eldridge, Tony Marchant and Mark Ravenhill. New writing development included the premieres of modern classics such as Mark Ravenhill's *Shopping and F***ing*, Conor McPherson's *This Lime Tree Bower*, Naomi Wallace's *Slaughter City* and Martin McDonagh's *The Pillowman*.

Since 2000, new British plays have included Laura Wade's London debut *Young Emma*, commissioned for the Finborough Theatre; two one-woman shows by Miranda Hart; James Graham's *Albert's Boy* with Victor Spinetti; Sarah Grochala's *S27*; Peter Nichols' *Lingua Franca*, which transferred Off-Broadway; and West End transfers for Joy Wilkinson's *Fair*; Nicholas de Jongh's *Plague Over England*; and Jack Thorne's *Fanny and Faggot*. The late Miriam Karlin made her last stage appearance in *Many Roads to Paradise* in 2008. UK premieres of foreign plays have included Brad Fraser's *Wolfboy*; Lanford Wilson's *Sympathetic Magic*; Larry Kramer's *The Destiny of Me*; Tennessee Williams' *Something Cloudy, Something Clear*; the English premiere of Robert McLellan's Scots language classic, *Jamie the Saxt*; and three West End transfers – Frank McGuinness' *Gates of Gold* with William Gaunt and John Bennett; Joe DiPietro's *F***ing Men*; and Craig Higginson's *Dream of the Dog* with Dame Janet Suzman.

Rediscoveries of neglected work – most commissioned by the Finborough Theatre – have included the first London revivals of Rolf Hochhuth's *Soldiers* and *The Representative*; both parts of Keith Dewhurst's *Lark Rise to Candleford*; *The Women's War*, an evening of original suffragette plays; *Etta Jenks* with Clarke Peters and Daniela Nardini; Noël Coward's first play, *The Rat Trap*; Charles Wood's *Jingo* with Susannah Harker; Emlyn Williams' *Accolade*; Lennox Robinson's *Drama at Inish* with Celia Imrie and Paul O'Grady; John Van Druten's *London Wall* which transferred to St James's Theatre; and J. B. Priestley's *Cornelius* which transferred to a sell out Off Broadway run in New York City.

Music Theatre has included the new (premieres from Grant Olding, Charles Miller, Michael John LaChuisa, Adam Guettel, Andrew Lippa, Paul Scott Goodman, and Adam Gwon's *Ordinary Days* which transferred to the West End) and the old (the UK premiere of Rodgers and Hammerstein's *State Fair* which also transferred to the West End), and the acclaimed 'Celebrating British Music Theatre' series, reviving forgotten British musicals.

The Finborough Theatre won *The Stage* Fringe Theatre of the Year Award in 2011, *London Theatre Reviews'* Empty Space Peter Brook Award in 2010 and 2012, the Empty Space Peter Brook Award's Dan Crawford Pub Theatre Award in 2005 and 2008, the Empty Space Peter Brook Mark Marvin Award in 2004, and swept the board with eight awards at the 2012 OffWestEnd Awards including Best Artistic Director and Best Director for the second year running. *Accolade* was named Best Fringe Show of 2011 by *Time Out*. It is the only unsubsidised theatre ever to be awarded the Pearson Playwriting Award (now the Channel 4 Playwrights Scheme) nine times. Three bursary holders (Laura Wade, James Graham and Anders Lustgarten) have also won the Catherine Johnson Award for Pearson Best Play.

www.finboroughtheatre.co.uk

The Finborough Theatre has the support of the Channel 4 Playwrights' Scheme, sponsored by Channel 4 Television and supported by The Peggy Ramsay Foundation.

Supported by

The Richard Carne Trust richardcarnetrust.org

The Finborough Theatre is a member of the Independent Theatre Council, the Society of Independent Theatres, Musical Theatre Network, The Friends of Brompton Cemetery and The Earl's Court Society www.earlscourtsociety.org.uk

Mailing
Email admin@finboroughtheatre.co.uk or give your details to our Box Office staff to join our free email list. If you would like to be sent a free season leaflet every three months, just include your postal address and postcode.

Follow Us Online
www.facebook.com/FinboroughTheatre
www.twitter.com/finborough

Feedback
We welcome your comments, complaints and suggestions. Write to Finborough Theatre, 118 Finborough Road, London SW10 9ED or email us at admin@finboroughtheatre.co.uk

Playscripts
Many of the Finborough Theatre's plays have been published and are on sale from our website.

Finborough Theatre T Shirts
Finborough Theatre T Shirts are now on sale from the Box Office, available in Small and Medium £7.00.

Smoking is not permitted in the auditorium and the use of cameras and recording equipment is strictly prohibited.

In accordance with the requirements of the Royal Borough of Kensington and Chelsea:

1. The public may leave at the end of the performance by all doors and such doors must at that time be kept open.

2. All gangways, corridors, staircases and external passageways intended for exit shall be left entirely free from obstruction whether permanent or temporary. 3. Persons shall not be permitted to stand or sit in any of the gangways intercepting the seating or to sit in any of the other gangways.

The Finborough Theatre is licensed by the Royal Borough of Kensington and Chelsea to The Steam Industry, a registered charity and a company limited by guarantee. Registered in England and Wales no. 3448268. Registered Charity no. 1071304. Registered Office: 118 Finborough Road, London SW10 9ED. The Steam Industry is under the overall Artistic Direction of Phil Willmott. www.philwillmott.co.uk

OBAMA-OLOGY

Aurin Squire

OBAMA-OLOGY

OBERON BOOKS
LONDON

WWW.OBERONBOOKS.COM

First published in 2014 by Oberon Books Ltd

521 Caledonian Road, London N7 9RH

Tel: +44 (0.) 20 7607 3637 / Fax: +44 (0.) 20 7607 3629

e-mail: info@oberonbooks.com

www.oberonbooks.com

A catalogue record for this book is available from the British
Library.

PB ISBN: 978-1-78319-204-5

E ISBN: 978-1-78319-703-3

Cover image by David Wagner

Printed, bound and converted
by CPI Group (UK.) Ltd, Croydon, CR0 4YY.

Visit www.oberonbooks.com to read more about all our books
and to buy them. You will also find features, author interviews and
news of any author events, and you can sign up for e-newsletters
so that you're always first to hear about our new releases.

Character Tracks

This was initially conceived of as a four-actor ensemble play. But I have seen as few as four and as many as 10 actors used to create the world and its characters. Some casting flexibility can be employed, but this play should have no fewer than four actors and probably no more than 12.

CLEVELAND TRACK ONE – early 20s, Black male
1. WARREN – young, idealistic, political wonk

CLEVELAND TRACK TWO – late 20s, Black female
1. INSTRUCTOR #1 – helpful campaign guide. Narrator
2. BARBARA – hard-nosed field organizer in East Cleveland
3. RESIDENT #1 – annoyed Cleveland resident
4. CECE – single mother looking to change her life
5. CAITS – frustrated and troubled young woman
6. NEIGHBOR – older woman on the block
7. MOM – Warren's mom

CLEVELAND TRACK THREE– late 20s, White male
1. INSTRUCTOR #2 – helpful campaign guide
2. SAM – East Cleveland Field Organizer
3. RESIDENT #2 – apathetic Cleveland resident
4. COP 1 – nervous, rookie officer
5. COP 2 – surly veteran traffic policeman
6. NIGHT COP – jittery rookie officer
7. BRAD – perky campaign volunteer
8. DAD – Warren's Dad (off-stage.)

CLEVELAND TRACK FOUR – late 20s, White female
1. INSTRUCTOR #3 – helpful campaign guide
2. LAURA – East Cleveland campaign director
3. RESIDENT #3 – Stepford-type wife
4. STORE CLERK – racist store clerk
5. LAINEY – perky campaign volunteer

SETTING

The play takes place in the rental cars, street corners,
and campaign offices of Cleveland during the 2008 election.

PRODUCTION NOTES

This is Brechtian comedic theatre. The transitions should match
the brevity of this tone. The props should be minimal.

The "Instructors" serve as guides for Warren throughout the play.

For door-to-door campaign scenes, an actual stand-alone door
is not necessary. A simple spot of light to emphasize an opening
should suffice. For door knocking, someone in the ensemble can
provide sound effect by hitting a staff against the floor. An on-stage
prop table might be an efficient and clear way to present the items
to the audience. When finished with a prop, an actor can simply
put the item back on the prop table. Warren's suitcase is something
which can exist on-stage throughout the play. He lives from that
suitcase and can pull things from it when needed.

ACT ONE

SCENE ONE: THE JOURNEY BEGINS

WARREN packs a suitcase.

INSTRUCTORS: Dear volunteer, this is bigger than you.

WARREN: I am ready.

INSTRUCTOR #1: Are you prepared to travel?

WARREN: Wherever you need me.

INSTRUCTOR #2: What about a swing state?

WARREN: Sunny, beautiful Florida? The shores of
North Carolina?

INSTRUCTOR #1: You're a bit young to be an official,
paid staffer.

WARREN: Yes, but this campaign is about the youth and
I want to be a part of this moment. Now I know I'm very
young but I graduated with honors at the top of my class.
And I still believe.

INSTRUCTORS: Still believe in…

WARREN: America. Its people. This campaign.

INSTRUCTOR #1: You're right. You are very young.

INSTRUCTOR #2: Being a campaign staffer means being
the face of a candidate.

INSTRUCTOR #2: Why do you want to be the face?

WARREN: I think this election is about more than Obama.

INSTRUCTOR #3: Oh really?

WARREN: It's about what this country is and what it will be.

INSTRUCTOR #3: And what is that?

WARREN: I don't know. But I want to find out. And I'm packed. I'm fired up and ready to go.

INSTRUCTOR #1: Well okay, Warren. You got your sun tan lotion?

WARREN: Check.

INSTRUCTOR #2: Swim trunks?

WARREN: Double check.

INSTRUCTOR #3: Then follow our instructions and get ready for sunny, beautiful… Ohio. East Cleveland. You familiar with the city?

WARREN: I think Dante wrote about it.

LIGHTS SHIFT. WARREN is driving a rental car in East Cleveland. SAM and BARBARA are passengers.

SAM: You're excited?

WARREN: Yes, I always wanted to come to East Cleveland. We are doing something important. Making history, you know?

BARBARA: *(Surly.)* Mmmmhmmmm.

SAM: Now we're going to be moving fast on this, Warren. You're sort of coming in the middle of things but we're glad you could fly out here on such short notice after graduating.

WARREN: Yes, and I'm not afraid of jumping in. I'm a fast learner.

BARBARA: Mmmmhmmmm.

SAM: I know you'll do a great job. You'll be taking over for Phil who had to take a leave of absence.

WARREN: What happened to him?

SAM: Gee...hmmm, I think Phil just needed a breather.

BARBARA: Yes. Phil fucked up. Take this exit. We do a lot of work with black churches in the area. What kind of church do you go to?

WARREN: Actually...ahh, no. I don't do church.

BARBARA: You don't do church? Did your parents forget to take you?

WARREN: Oh no, they...they certainly didn't forget to beat me over the head with the Bible. I just learned how to dodge their loving, Christian blows and find my own way. BUT I love and respect all kinds of religions.

BARBARA: So what does that mean? You're an atheist?

SAM: You don't have to answer that, Warren.

BARBARA: Sounds like another Phil.

WARREN: Well I promise not to fill Phil's shoes.

The joke lands flat.

SAM: I know you're going to do a great job. Right Barbara?

BARBARA: A lot of times we work 18 hours a day. No time off.

WARREN: I will cancel all my Brazilian wax appointments, Barbara.

BARBARA: 51%. Take a right at the light.

WARREN: What's that?

SAM: The target we need to vote.

WARREN: Why that amount?

BARBARA: Because that's the target. Look, we don't have time to –

SAM: – Warren, East Cleveland is a predominantly black neighborhood so there's no competition from the other side for voters. All we have to do is find a way to push people to the polls. If we get a large enough percentage here, then we win all of Cleveland by a landslide. If we win Cleveland by a large enough margin we can counteract Cincinnati, which is conservative. And then if we off-set Cincy, we win Ohio. And if we win Ohio, then we win…

WARREN: Everything.

SAM: Exactly. East Cleveland is the tipping point of the political universe. We take this area, we take the country.

BARBARA: And if we lose this neighborhood, then we just screwed up a lifetime of work. Years of sweat, tears, and blood…for some of us.

SAM: 51%. Right now we're tracking at significantly below that in most Black neighborhoods. Particularly in the ward you'll be managing. Your job will be to help bump up the early voting numbers, making sure voters have rides to and from the polls, and patrolling the streets.

BARBARA: Why did you want this job?

WARREN: It's a great opportunity. It's history.

BARBARA: So was Janet Jackson flashing her titty in the Super Bowl. But why did you want to be a part of *this* history?

WARREN: I don't know. The same reason as everyone else: to matter.

BARBARA: You're not understanding the question. Pull up here to this house. *(WARREN pulls up and parks the car.)* You're going to be in the community. That means training the locals, knocking on doors, and working with the people. 'Black people.'

WARREN: Great. My parents are 'Black people.'

SAM: Funny.

BARBARA: Corny. College boy, what do you know about these people?

SAM: I know you're going to do a great job. Be sure to make friends. Make lots and lots of friends. Happy to have you on board.

BARBARA: Don't fuck this up.

SCENE 2: OFFICE TRAINING

INSTRUCTOR #3: Office. Wedged in the corner of a shopping plaza between a check-cash store and a discount dress shop is your headquarters. Occasionally you walk inside at 7 a.m. and find workers curled up underneath the tables waking up from a 3 hour nap to go back to work. In the first 24 hours we expect you to get up to speed on training people for phone banks, door-to-door work, tabulation, and setting up GOTV: the "Get Out the Vote" drive. Each block has a community leader whose house serves as an organizing beacon for quick bursts of action. Get people to like you.

Split scene between SAM/BARBARA, and WARREN. WARREN is talking to a volunteer.

BARBARA: I don't like him.

WARREN: Hello, I'm Warren Clayton. And I am so happy that you decided to show up. Even if it's in your pajamas and flip flops. Now I think we're all getting a feel for each other but I just want you to know that I relate to the...struggle and the urban blight, I mean plight. Plight. Okay let me just take out my roll...

SAM: ...you'll grow to like him.

BARBARA: He's another one of those uppity, Black, political tourists looking to build his resume. We should've hired someone from the community. Let me make a few phone calls and I can find someone.

SAM: You find someone and then what?

BARBARA: We go to Laura as a united front and get him shipped off to some other place that's not as important as this time, this area.

SAM: There aren't a lot of people who have his skill set. He learned everything we threw at him.

WARREN: Worried about the GOTV software? I can help you. Computers are easy for me.

BARBARA: People aren't computers. I just don't see people relating to him.

SAM: I relate to him.

BARBARA: Sam, you'd relate to a potted plant. It's your White liberal guilt. You 'relate' so that you can pretend like you fit in. You see moss hanging from a tree and read its aura.

SAM: That was one time and I was tipsy.

BARBARA: And you use words like 'tipsy!' You're too nice to guys like Warren and it's because you think he's a precious minority.

SAM: What are you talking about?

BARBARA: Sam, I know you care. But you treat Warren like a lot of White liberals do: like delicate little flowers that must not be put under any stress or have their integrity questioned. And that's how we end up with people like Clarence Thomas: Unqualified, narcissistic buffoons who have no connection to the community, to history, or sense of obligation.

WARREN: *(Talking to someone leaving.)* Uh, excuse me…where are you going? If you're looking for the bathroom… *(VOLUNTEER is gone.)* Must've had an emergency.

INSTRUCTOR #3: Your first wave of volunteers will be your toughest… There may be some 'language issues' but handle it with a cool, calm, professional manner.

WARREN: What? No we don't have a break yet. Now I've got it. Daily roll call. Here we go…hmmm… *(Reading name.)* La-quil-vel-ve-ta? *(Listening.)* What? It's pronounced how? Oh, how about I call you…Velma? Now if you could just quiet down a bit…um please. Quiet down!! Hmmm…look how do you expect to get ahead if you can't pay attention for 30 seconds? Listen, I am your friend.

BARBARA: Talking to them like they're barbarians in the wild. Is this how he's gonna relate to Black people? Church-going, Cleveland-raised, direct, no-bullshit folks.

WARREN: Why don't we take a break? We got donuts in the back. Go…shove food in your faces. Go go go. *(To INSTRUCTOR.)* What is this?

INSTRUCTOR #3: This is America. Land of the free.

SAM: He'll adjust. Just like the training. He's a quick learner.

BARBARA: You can't learn soul.

SAM: And if I said that about him you'd call me racist.

BARBARA: Yes, but I've earned the right to judge him. You haven't. These people will look at him and see a shallow, snobby Black traitor. And they'll associate our campaign with that type of person. And it's this very same suspicion in the Black community that Obama has fought against his whole career. You can do whatever you want, Sam, and no one will judge all White people by that. But a Black man in this city today has to be held at a higher standard because everyone is going to come after him. A Black man has to better. And he isn't.

SAM: Barbara, don't you think you're being a bit…relentless.

BARBARA: I just want the best.

SAM: And maybe his best is something he'll have to discover. But he's not going to get there if you stomp on him.

WARREN: These aren't residents. They're survivors.

SAM: Let's give him a week. See if he meets his outreach targets, gets volunteers to come out for him, and if people are connecting to him.

SCENE THREE: 'X' MARKS THE SPOT

INSTRUCTOR #1: The street. This is your stomping ground, volunteers. You have to own your turf like its tribal land. All those in-office scenarios can only give you a taste of the real thing. Okay, now let's knock on some doors.

WARREN is walking around the neighborhood with clipboard of voter information.

INSTRUCTOR #2: You want to check the address before exiting the car. If you don't see your house there is a good chance the house was knocked down, foreclosed, or abandoned. Like many houses around the country. Now if you are well-dressed, some residents might yell things at you. Things like...

INSTRUCTOR #1: Uncle Tom!

INSTRUCTOR #3: They might also yell things like 'punk!'

INSTRUCTOR #2: Retard!

INSTRUCTOR #1: Do-Boy!

INSTRUCTOR #2: Bitch!

INSTRUCTOR #3: Faggot!

INSTRUCTOR #1: Faggot-ass nigga!

WARREN: And I'm supposed to just –

INSTRUCTOR #2: – stay cool and calm in those situations. Keep a professional tone and keep it moving...bitch. Just kidding.

WARREN: Ok. Cool and calm. Keep it moving.

WARREN knocks. Then he pushes doorbell. He pushes doorbell again and is shocked. He rubs his hand.

INSTRUCTOR #3: Most doorbells won't be working and can give a nasty shock from the old wiring so don't even bother trying. If someone pulls a weapon on you...

WARREN puts his hands in the air.

INSTRUCTOR #1: Immediately, but slowly back away from the property. But don't turn your back to the owner.

WARREN backs away.

INSTRUCTOR #2: And volunteers: never go inside someone's house. Attempted kidnapping and volunteers being held hostage have happened. Your safety should come first.

WARREN moves on to another house.

INSTRUCTOR #3: And before you knock on each door remember...

INSTRUCTORS: Smile. Have fun and make friends. You are representing hope.

WARREN knocks on the door. Resident, Black female, doesn't open the door.

RESIDENT #1: WHO IS IT?!?!

WARREN: Hi, ma'am? My name is Warren Clayton and –

RESIDENT #1: Who the fuck is that?!?

WARREN: ...tha-that's me. Ma'am. And what's your name?

RESIDENT #1: What's my name? My name is Diana Motherfuckin' Ross. What the fuck does it matter what my name is? Do I know you like that?

WARREN: Uh... I'm with the Obama campaign.

RESIDENT #1: Oh, Lord. Get your toilet paper out cause it's diarrhoea time on this bullshit.

WARREN: No, ma'am. It is not diarrhea time. This will only take a second.

RESIDENT #1: You got Obama out there with you?

WARREN: Only in spirit. I was looking for a Eunis Ray?
Are you –

RESIDENT #1: Nah, nigga. Have a nice day –

WARREN: – well ma'am I would like to leave you with some
lit –

RESIDENT #1: – nigga, I said have a nice day!

INSTRUCTOR #3: *(To VOLUNTEERS.)* The key to these door-to-
door campaigns is persistence. You will get rejections. Just
mark them down as 'not home' and we will get back to
them. Let's try another door.

WARREN knocks on the door. Dog starts barking.

RESIDENT #2: *(Coming to door.)* Shut up! Sit! Fucking Christ,
this better not be a campaign worker knocking at my door.

Dog continues barking. Barks intermittently throughout.

WARREN: Hello, I was looking for a Mr. Frederick Jones.

RESIDENT #2: It's Fred. Fefe! Get back!

WARREN: *(Offering hand.)* Hi, Fred. My name is Warren
Clayton. How are you today?

RESIDENT #2: Aww shit, you're from one of those campaigns,
aren't you?

WARREN: I'm with the –

RESIDENT #2: – Well you're wasting your time cause I ain't
voting.

WARREN: Are you sure, sir? Because this is a really important
election –

RESIDENT #2: – they say that every year. This is important.
And ain't nothing changed. *(Yelling at dog.)* Hey, Fefe! Shut
the fuck up! *(Closing door.)* You have a nice day.

INSTRUCTOR #1: If someone says they're not voting you mark down 'not voting' and we'll try to get someone to speak with them over the phone. You don't have to do the work of a salesman. Let's try a nicer looking home.

WARREN knocks on another door. RESIDENT #3 is a female. Well-dressed, middle-class. Smiling.

RESIDENT #3: *(Swings door open.)* Good afternoon.

WARREN: Good afternoon ma'am. How are you doing?

RESIDENT #3: I'm fine. How are you?

INSTRUCTOR #2: You see: we are establishing a friendly jovial rapport with the resident. You introduce yourself.

WARREN: My name is Warren Clayton. What's your's?

RESIDENT #3: Beth Frazier.

WARREN: Well Miss Frazier…

RESIDENT #3: Mrs. Dr. Frazier.

WARREN: Mrs. Dr. Frazier I'm with the Obama campaign. And we are reaching out to the community to get people to vote early.

RESIDENT #3: I'm going the first day of early voting. This election is very very important to me.

WARREN: Well good. We're in agreement.

RESIDENT #3: Yes.

WARREN: And may I ask: are you voting for Obama?

RESIDENT #3: No, I'm not.

WARREN: Oh. Well may I ask why?

RESIDENT #3: Simple: we don't vote for Blacks in this house. Have a nice day.

INSTRUCTOR #2: Remember volunteers: persistence is the key. You will face many different types of people. But you can't take it personally. As much as you might want to, you just can not take it personally. Move on to the next door and keep knocking.

Beat.

ALL INSTRUCTORS: I said, you move on and keep knocking.

WARREN knocks on another door.

CECE: *(Entering.)* Hello?

WARREN: Oh, hi? How are you?

CECE: I'm fine. How are you?

WARREN: I'm... I've had better days. But still we must go on. Right...sister?

CECE: I guess.

WARREN: My name is Warren Clayton and I'm with the Obama campaign.

CECE: I'm CeCe.

WARREN: Hello CeCe. That is a lovely name. I was looking for Vanessa Robinson.

CECE: That's my mom. She at work.

WARREN: Oh okay. Let me just mark that down on the sheet... like so. Do you know when she'll be back so I can make a note of that?

CECE: She working a double shift so it'll probably be after midnight.

WARREN: Then maybe over the weekend, I can stop by again.

CECE: She working at that time as well. Maybe you can call her when she gets home.

WARREN: We're not allowed to call people that late, CeCe. But thank you. Would you like some paraphernalia?

CECE: What?

WARREN: Some Obama stuff. I got bumper stickers.

CECE: I don't have a bumper to stick it on.

WARREN: You can put it on a folder or your door.

CECE: Sure. Obama is cool.

WARREN: Oh, you think so, huh? CeCe, how old are you?

CECE: 27. I got two babies: Reggie and Jamaar.

WARREN: Umm…all right, thanks for sharing. You know I think you would make your boys proud if you could be a part of this historic moment: getting Barack Obama elected. How would you like that?

CECE: Sure. What can I do?

WARREN: Well the first thing you can do is vote. Have you registered?

CECE: No, can I still do that?

WARREN: You can and we can help you fill all that out. And you can also volunteer. I will just take out my new volunteer forms like so. And then I will ask you to fill this out. Easy.

WARREN puts new volunteer form on clipboard and hands it to her. CECE takes it and stands there for a moment.

CECE: Oh…well. I left my reading glasses inside.

WARREN: That's okay. I can wait right out here for you to go get them.

Beat.

WARREN: Is everything all right?

CECE: I don't think I'll be able to find them.
(Hands forms back.)

WARREN: You know what, that happens to me all the time.
I can fill this out for you with your permission.

CECE: Sure.

WARREN: Okay, I just need you to sign your name.

CECE: Well I don't have my glasses so why don't you sign it?

WARREN: I think that would be illegal.

CECE: Look, maybe this isn't going to work.

WARREN: *(Writes on form.)* No, no, no. How about this:
I can write your name in there, date it. And you can mark
it with an 'X.' It's what they would do in old days when
people couldn't...when they had to speed things up. X
marks the spot.

CECE takes the pen and marks the document with an 'X.'

SCENE 4: NUMBERS TALLY

*WARREN gathers piles of envelopes from a box and struggles out the
door. LAURA enters.*

INSTRUCTOR #1: Office. There are daily and weekly number
tallies for each headquarter, field team, and individual
organizer. As a staffer or volunteer, you are judged by
these numbers.

LAURA: Hi, Warren. Do you have a moment?

WARREN: I'm a bit stacked up and behind here.

LAURA: What's the hold up?

WARREN: I got stopped by the police again. Is there anything
you can do about that?

LAURA: No, we're all getting it.

WARREN: I think I'm getting it a bit more than others.

LAURA: As long as you have Obama stuff out or they see your car parked here you're being watched and monitored. Just part of the territory.

WARREN: Well that's why I'm behind and why I have to run.

LAURA: Your numbers are low.

WARREN: In what area?

LAURA: All of them. In your voter registration, early voter commitments, volunteer commitments, phone bank. Even your retention rate of volunteers is lower than the other staffers.

WARREN: I'm new. I don't know the area as well.

LAURA: We're taking a chance on you and we want to see you succeed.

WARREN: And I am. It's going to get better.

LAURA: How come over 90% of your volunteers don't come back?

WARREN: I'm just weeding out the weak.

LAURA: Are you sure you're not having a problem connecting with the people and East Cleveland?

WARREN: *(Dry and sarcastic.)* No, it's like a dream here. I can't believe how much this reminds me of home.

LAURA: I didn't know you were a vegetarian.

WARREN: Why would you know that?

LAURA: Cause some of the volunteers commented on that when they brought by food for the staff. They find it weird. And also the beads you wear...

WARREN: Mala beads.

LAURA: Mali? Like the country.

WARREN: Mala. It's for meditation. I'm a Buddhist.

LAURA: Some people think they're voodoo beads. It's very off-putting.

WARREN: I can wear the beads under my shirt.

LAURA: Thanks. Look I know it's not fair.

WARREN: Yeah, well who said anything about life being fair, right?

LAURA: That's the right attitude. You know I got a sister over in Iraq. Army mechanic. She emails me once a week and tells me all the fucked-up compromises she has to make to fit in with the boys.

WARREN: Women in the military have it rough.

LAURA: Yes, so you see what I'm saying.

WARREN: About what?

LAURA: Making compromises.

WARREN: In the army, yes. But we're not the army.

LAURA: I know that! Look, just try to fit in more.

WARREN: Fit in how?

LAURA: I don't know. For instance the way you speak.

WARREN: Yes, what is 'thy' problem with my elocution?

LAURA: You can try to talk more…earthy. Real.

WARREN: What do you think I'm speaking? Hobbit? I'm using real words.

LAURA: Try to talk more like the people you're speaking to.

WARREN: You want me to speak in Ebonics?

LAURA: I want you to relate to people. You have a degree in communications. So communicate.

WARREN: In Ebonics?

LAURA: In the…vernacular of your ancestors.

WARREN: Well let me 'axe' you sum'ing, how come you don't be speaking like that?

LAURA: Warren, you and I…are different. When they look at me they expect me to speak…

WARREN: Laura, both my grandmothers were maids. They worked their entire lives to buy a house and send the first in our lineage to college. And in turn, my parents worked hard to send me to the best schools, see the world, travel in the best circles. And I worked my ass off to always make the honors roll, get an academic scholarship to college, and prove that I belong with the best. And my father and mother, grandparents, and ancestors did not raise me up on their backs so that I could talk like a degenerate ghetto thug.

LAURA: Warren, it's that attitude that's creating this issue.

WARREN: That's excrement.

LAURA: Excuse me?

WARREN: My father would always tell me, "imagine you have a mouth full of excrement. Because every time you corrupt the language, you are corrupting thought itself." And while I do occasionally enjoy the fecal splatter that passes for music and culture these days I am a tourist, not a resident of Ghetto Fabulous, USA.

Beat.

WARREN: Now, I am Black enough to get stopped by the police. And I'm sure as hell Black enough to work on a campaign for the first African American who has a chance at being the leader of the free world.

LAURA: Well he won't have a chance at winning an election with your approach. Because your numbers are excrement.

And you're going to get flushed with them. I know
I'm tough but I want to see you do well.

WARREN: Things will come around. These are my kind of
people.

LAURA: But are you *their* kind?

SCENE FIVE: PARKING LOT

INSTRUCTOR #1: Car. Your rented motor vehicle is a place
of refuge. In the heat of a campaign, it is your floating
fortress.

WARREN GETS INTO HIS CAR

INSTRUCTOR #1: Be sure to outfit it with the appropriate glove
compartment snacks, drinks under the seat, and music in
the door pockets. Have at least a few T-shirts and pants for
quick changes when you don't have time to go back home.

*WARREN puts on a new T-shirt from the ground. He sprays on some
deodorant and smells himself.*

INSTRUCTOR #3: A lint roller and spray-on deodorant gives
you that fresh shower "je ne sais quoi" when you've been
going 'French' for a few days. When you are spending
hours in your car, the air will begin to develop that sour
stale scent. That's where Febreeze comes in handy. Just
cover your seats and floor in it once a day. And every once
and awhile, when you want to get away from the bustle of
the office it's nice to sit in your car, wrap a T-shirt around
your arm as a pillow and take a power nap.

*WARREN naps. POLICE OFFICER comes and taps on window.
WARREN wakes up and opens the door.*

COP #1: Is everything all right?

WARREN: …Yes, officer. Just taking a nap.

COP #1: License and registration.

WARREN: Why?

COP #1: Are you sassing me?

WARREN: Am I 'sassing you?' I don't know. Am I in a *Dick Tracy* cartoon?

COP #1: Sir, I'm going to need you to step out of the car.

WARREN gets out. The cop proceeds to pat WARREN down, take his license. BARBARA enters with camera phone as she tape records the exchange.

BARBARA: Officer, is there a problem?

COP #1: There won't be if your boy follows orders.

WARREN: Boy?

BARBARA: What is he being charged with?

WARREN: A nap in a parked car.

BARBARA: Warren, please –

WARREN: – please nothing. I'm not doing anything.

COP #1: This is a traffic stop.

WARREN: But I'm not in traffic!

COP #1: You're getting smart with me, aren't you?

WARREN: No, I'm not getting smart. I'm getting obvious! I am in a parked car in a parking lot. If this was a 'traffic stop' then I would have to a.) be in traffic and b.) moving in a vehicle so that you could 'stop' me. Since I'm not in traffic and was already stopped then this can't be a traffic stop. This is a nap stop. You are preventing me from napping. And if you think about it, somewhere out there real crimes are being committed. Brutal, heinous crimes that you could be stopping. But instead you are here interrupting my nap. To me that's not smart at all. It's obvious. An obvious abortion of common sense.

INSTRUCTOR #3: Dear volunteers: sometimes police officers don't like being told what is obvious. Especially when you use phrases like an 'abortion of common sense.' You could end up handcuffed to a steering wheel. Or dragged from your car and wrestled to the ground.

WARREN: Or getting a ticket. A big fat one.

COP exits.

BARBARA: I have never seen you speak with that much passion. For a moment when I walked up I thought you had snagged your first volunteer of the day.

WARREN: Now who's getting smart?

BARBARA: Not smart. Just obvious. You ready to throw in the towel yet?

WARREN: Ever since I got here you've been looking at me like I'm a sellout.

BARBARA: You're not a sellout. You're just weak. And sheltered. And spoiled. And bougie. And not helpful to the cause. When you go out there you are the face of the campaign and you don't get that. You don't walk the walk or talk the talk.

WARREN: So you think I should talk like I'm from the ghetto?

BARBARA: You know the story of when Obama first ran for office?

WARREN: Yeah, he got his ass kicked by Bobby Rush.

BARBARA: He was right out of Harvard. And had all these big ideas about community organizing, innovating the black civil rights movement and bringing the people up to his level of a Harvard lawyer. He would sit there at neighborhood meetings with his head flung back and his chin up, looking like Napoleon. And he was called a sell-out, Uncle Tom, uppity, and an Oreo. He was hated. And he lost. He had to learn how to talk to his own.

WARREN: In Ebonics?

BARBARA: He had to get in their lives, go to cookouts, and yes occasionally raise his voice like a Sunday minister to get the crowd moving. Call and response. He had to compromise. This is politics. You think it's a shame to speak like what Laura and Sam glorify as the 'great negro dialect.' But it's not our glory or our shame. It's just another way of reaching out.

WARREN: My parents didn't raise me to pretend like I'm from the 'hood.'

I hate it when educated Blacks fake an accent and start swinging their voice in a sing-songy cadence, quoting Negro spirituals like they're from the fields.

BARBARA: House slave vs. field slave. Blacks have been fighting the same battle with each other for hundreds of years.

WARREN: Don't give me that Malcolm X bullshit. I just got a ticket for taking a nap in a parked car. I am aware that I'm Black.

BARBARA: This isn't about just being aware of your Blackness. It's about the shades of color in our own community. Do you embrace all of the differences or just think your way is the best? Because the field is also a part of you. Not just one side. And if we're going to work together we have to embrace as many different shades of us as possible. Dark-skinned, light-skinned, biracial, high-yellow, redbone, college educated, GED, dropped out of school, nappy, kinky, braided, field house, hood, suburbs, classroom, White House. It's not Ebonics. It's Obama-ology. That's how you relate to people. You don't have to beat people over the head with your education nor do you have to hide it. You use it to bring all the different parts together.

WARREN: Well that's very poetic and grand sounding, Barbara. But I think it's a little unrealistic to ask me to be responsible for healing the entire continuum of race problems in America.

BARBARA: You don't get it. That's why you got to be twice as good as everyone else. This is why I knew you weren't ready. You thought this was just about running a campaign and getting the right numbers. But it's about changing people's hearts who have been beaten down.

WARREN: How do you do that?

BARBARA: Maybe by changing your own heart about them. And figuring out why you're here.

WARREN: I told you why I was here: this is history.

BARBARA: History doesn't motivate people. It's passion. And then passionate people are the ones who make history. Where is your soul? Where is your passion?

SCENE SIX: OFFICE FEVER

INSTRUCTOR #3: *(Sniffling.)* Office. Around the middle part of the campaign, after working 90 hour weeks, eating junk food, shaking hundreds of hands, and drinking buckets of coffee, the immune system breaks down. And all at once, the office becomes a sick bay of disgruntled political refugees. And you start thinking of home. Your bed. Fresh vegetables. Your family. You keep going, looking for the light.

CECE walks in and is greeted by a coughing and bleary-eyed SAM.

SAM: Good morning *(Coughing.)* can I help you?

CECE: Yes, I was here to see Mr. Warren.

SAM: You're a *(Coughing.)* ...a volunteer?

CECE: Yes.

SAM: From East Cleveland?

WARREN enters, coughing.

CECE: Hi, Mr. Warren?

WARREN: Yes. Hello, can I help you?

CECE: Hey, remember me? I'm CeCe. You signed me up to volunteer.

WARREN: Yes, Sam. This is one of my volunteers...from the community. A community volunteer that I signed up...who actually showed up.

SAM: *(Exiting.)* I knew you could do it. Turning the corner.

WARREN: You know it. So CeCe... I'll give you a brief walk-through of Get Out the Vote, the GOTV phone banks, and then door-to-door volunteering, okay? Now we have a script that we hand all of...but you –

CECE: – yeah. My glasses.

WARREN: You forgot them. Of course. Okay, let's just try talking this through. Numbers. Can you...see those?

CECE: Yes.

WARREN: So I'm going to help you out. You'll dial the number and I will tell you the name of the resident. They will pick up and answer and you will say...

CECE: Hey.

WARREN: Hello. Or good morning, or good afternoon. Not 'hey.'

CECE: Good morning.

WARREN: Right. You say your name and who you're with the Obama campaign.

CECE: "My name is CeCe Robinson and I'm with the Obama campaign. Are you going to vote for him?"

WARREN: Not so fast. You ask them first if they're going to vote. If they say no, you want to stress the importance of voting.

CECE: And what's that?

WARREN: What's the importance of voting? It's letting your voice be heard. If they are Black, they are underrepresented. If they are poor or middle class they are underrepresented and their voice needs to be heard. If they are a woman, a minority, a young adult, a single mother, have lived paycheck to paycheck, found themselves in debt, if they ever had a problem with seeing a doctor, paying medical bills. If they are getting screwed over in this country, then what?

CECE: They are underrepresented and their voice needs to be heard?

WARREN: Right. And ask them about what issues are important to them. Now you move on to asking them if they're voting for Obama. Yes. No. Undecided. If it's a strong 'no' then you thank them and hang up. If it's an 'undecided' then bring me on the phone and I'll talk to them. If it's a 'yes' then you want to ask them if they're voting early. You want to emphasize that it's important that they vote early. Lines are a huge problem on election day. Especially in black neighborhoods. We're trying to get our community out early and often. If they're going to vote early ask them if they need a ride. We can connect them with rides in our carpool. You got all that?

CECE: Not really.

WARREN: Well I can write... *(Stops himself.)* you're just going to have to try. You'll get better with practice.

CECE: This seems complicated.

WARREN: That's because it's new.

CECE: Maybe I should go home and, you know, practice.

WARREN: *(Aside to INSTRUCTOR.)* If they leave before they do any work, they'll never come back. *(To CECE.)* You're just having cold feet.

CECE: My feet are fine.

WARREN: Figure of speech. It just means you're nervous.

CECE: I don't know...maybe I could take one of these scripts and go practice at home.

WARREN: Doesn't work that way. We aren't allowed to let people take scripts home.

CECE: I'm feeling a bit tired.

WARREN: What about letting your voice be heard?

CECE: That voice shit don't mean nothing to me.

WARREN: Wait, wait... CeCe. Before you go, can you answer one question: why did you come down here?

CECE: Cause you asked me to volunteer.

WARREN: Yeah, but I ask a hundred people a day if they'll help out. Most say no, some slam the door in my face, some cuss me out, call me names, say I'm...the point is that you were one of the few who answered the call. Right? You made the effort. You got out the door and traveled down here in the middle of the day. Why?

CECE: I want Obama to win.

WARREN: Yes, but why did you answer the call on that day, at that time, from a perfect stranger knocking on your door?

CECE: I was sitting at home last night and your office called to remind me to stop by. To be honest, Mr. Warren, I wasn't going to come in. I should be looking for work, you know. But then I thought of my sons. They're going to grow up and ask what I did when I had the chance to do something. I didn't want to say nothing. I wanted to be able to tell them that I did something. That their mom is worth something. And so that's why I'm here.

WARREN: Then you speak from that. Forget what I said. You speak from that passion. Let people know that they're worth something. And I'll be right here. Helping you out.

SCENE SEVEN: CONVENIENCE STORE

WARREN walks down the aisle of a convenience store. He's trailed by STORE CLERK, who is tracking his every move.

INSTRUCTOR #1: Convenience Store. After your first good day it's important to reward yourself. And there is a place to find fluorescent serenity. The convenience store across the street from the headquarters. It's important to find those small pauses in the campaign to decompress a bit.

STORE CLERK: Excuse me, can I help you?

WARREN: I am just enjoying the lovely hum of electric lights, glass refrigerators, and automatic doors.

INSTRUCTOR #1: *(Hands gossip magazine to WARREN.)* Roam the aisle, peruse trashy magazines…

WARREN: *(Reading gossip and laughing.)* Peruse I will.

INSTRUCTOR #1: Enjoy a ribald piece of gossip about the famous and favored…

WARREN: Scandalous. Look at these trifling-ass… *(About to say something but censors himself.)* …people!

INSTRUCTOR #1: Be sure to shield the few personal minutes you have from reading any topical news magazines.

WARREN: I get enough of that on the campaign.

INSTRUCTOR #1: Don't read about the wars, the melting ice caps, or the recent global catastrophe.

WARREN: What recent catastrophe?

INSTRUCTOR #1: Something involving sub-prime mortgages and devastating financial hemorrhaging.

STORE CLERK: Are you sure there's not something I can help you with, sir?

WARREN: Hold on a second *(To STORE CLERK.)* Yes?

STORE CLERK: I was saying 'are you sure you don't need help finding anything?'

WARREN: *(Looks at name tag.)* Janice, dear? I think I can manage to find my way. But I will fire off a rescue flare if I find myself lost at sea, ok? Namaste. Ta-ta. Scram!

Beat.

WARREN: She's not going away, is she?

After a moment, WARREN hands the magazine back to the INSTRUCTOR.

WARREN: I shall return.

WARREN gets in his car and drives.

WARREN: There's got to be another place to decompress. Maybe I'll just drive around and see the other parts of Cleveland.

INSTRUCTOR #1: Dear volunteer, that is not recommended.

WARREN: Why not?

INSTRUCTOR #1: While Obama's name on your car is a shield from gangs, it is a bulls-eye for cops. Let's look in at a few re-enacted traffic stops. Cop stop!

COP #2 plays a variety of different officers in this next section.

COP #2: That was an illegal turn.

WARREN: I didn't see that. But okay.

COP #2 just stares at WARREN who stares and slumps down.

INSTRUCTOR #1: You see that: cool and calm. Like Obama. Cop stop.

COP #2: Why is your trunk so low?

WARREN: It's filled with campaign lit.

COP #2: It looks…suspicious.

WARREN: Officer, I'd like to give you an Obama T-shirt and bumper sticker. As a gift. From me to you.

INSTRUCTOR #1: Good dispensation of humor. Nice job.

COP #2: …you're funny. Pop the trunk.

WARREN: The trunk is popped. Take a few free bumper stickers and hats.

INSTRUCTOR #1: Excellent job of letting them walk all over you. Cop stop.

COP #2: What is that stuff in your backseat?

WARREN: Officer… *(Suppressing anger.)* It's just boxes of voting data.

COP #2: We'll see about that. Could you please open the back door?

WARREN: Do you wish to search the boxes? Because I believe you're going to need something called a 'search warrant.' You know what that is right? A search warrant means getting judicial approval for digging through my stuff.

Beat.

WARREN: Just kidding. Just a little joke I like to call 'my constitutional rights.'

INSTRUCTOR #1: Funny. Although try to stay away from political satire.

WARREN: The door is unlocked.

INSTRUCTOR #1: Learn to find ways to decompress and use humor.

WARREN: I don't know how much more of this I can take.

INSTRUCTOR #1: Remember volunteers, there is a thin line between being a college-educated uppity Black New Yorker, and being a crying wreck in an East Cleveland jail.

SCENE EIGHT: NIGHT BEFORE

INSTRUCTOR #2: Office. Night before early voting. After months of field canvassing, candidate canvassing, phone canvassing, stealth marketing, and voter persuasion these are the last few hours before the early election D-Day, when personal desires and fears creep out into the quiet lull.

LAURA speaks before the staff. BARBARA is checking her phone and has her jacket on.

LAURA: We've worked hard for this moment but it's not over yet. We gotta get out, knock on doors, and remind people to vote early. Every year it seems like we have less voting machines in this neighborhood and of poorer quality. So we have to emphasize that the earlier they vote, the less wait, and the more likely their voice gets heard. Now as a reward for all your hard work, you get off early tonight. It's only 12:40. Enjoy.

WARREN: Thank you, Pharaoh. Hey Barbara, it's not even 1 a.m.

BARBARA: Hallelujah.

WARREN: I don't know what to do with all this free time. You want to go get some Korean food?

BARBARA: You want to have dinner with me?

WARREN: Sure. We started off on the wrong foot but...things are changing. And I have a favor I want to ask you and I figured I might have a better chance over a meal.

BARBARA: Can't. I have a date.

WARREN: How do you have free time for a date?

BARBARA: This is our last night of freedom and I ain't spending it with you. I'm going out for a drink with my husband.

WARREN: You have a husband?!?

BARBARA: Yes, college boy! So you're going to have to drink alone. And by the way there's nothing to toast yet. You're still lagging behind the rest of us.

WARREN: I'll catch up.

BARBARA: You seem pretty cocky for someone whose numbers are in, what, second to last place in the office?

WARREN: Third to last. New numbers just came out this evening.

BARBARA: Congratulations, Warren. I will see you tomorrow.

BARBARA exits and LAURA enters with her eyeballs glued to her phone as she's reading something. She almost runs into WARREN.

WARREN: Working and walking is a health hazard.

LAURA: Huh?

WARREN: Nothing. You're checking the office numbers from your phone?

LAURA: No, I was just trying to get some information about… something.

WARREN: Laura, you gotta take at least an hour or two off from this or you'll kill yourself.

LAURA: Right. You going out?

WARREN: Yes. *(Thinking.)* And you're just the person I've been wanting to talk to. How about we grab some Korean food?

LAURA: Nah, I'm trying to watch my figure. How about whiskey?

WARREN: Sure. One quick drink.

LIGHTS SHIFT to a bar.

WARREN: Or four. Thanks for coming out with me, Laura. I wanted to ask –

LAURA: – Warren, I just want to apologize to you for the Ebonics suggestion. I'm under a lot of pressure and some times I don't say the most constructive things. So are we... cool?

WARREN: Cool, calm, and copacetic. So, Laura –

LAURA: – Look at this place: sticky floors, dirty men, and $3 shots. Want another?

WARREN: Want another what? Dirty man or shot?

LAURA: What would you do with a dirty man?

WARREN: The real question is what wouldn't I do?

LAURA: Warren, I didn't know you are...batting for the other team.

WARREN: How would you? I left my nipple tassels and feather boa behind in New York.

LAURA: No, it's just that...well. Um, your parents must be so proud and –

WARREN: *(To himself.)* – Not really, but no big deal. Laura, I wanted to ask –

LAURA: How could they not be?

WARREN: My parents are very conservative. In fact they might be the only people I know who are voting Republican in this election.

LAURA: But still, they should be pleased with you. You're an intelligent young man who is politically active, out, and proud.

WARREN: Hey...don't change the subject. I wanted you to look at these numbers for...

LAURA: God, if you weren't gay... *(Suggestive look.)*

WARREN: What?

LAURA: Nothing. Who said that? Not me. We have ethical rules in this campaign about that sort of…thing.

WARREN: Right.

LAURA: And you're sure that you strictly, only…play for the other team?

WARREN: Yes.

LAURA: Mazel tov. So happy for you. Well. Can you drive me home?

WARREN: Now? I thought we were going to have the chance to chat.

LAURA: *(Not interested.)* Oh okay. Fine. So how are things going?

WARREN: *(Handing folder to her.)* Doing a lot better. Now what do you see when you look at these numbers?

LAURA: I thought we were taking the night off from that.

WARREN: Just this one exception. Tell me what you think…

LAURA: *(Opening folder and looking at data sheets.)* They look pretty good. Well Warren, I'm kind of tired –

WARREN: – I have a star volunteer. Her name is CeCe. These are her stats. She's not too great on the phone but she's a beast on the streets. She knocks on doors, gets people at their level, she really seems to get it.

LAURA: Warren –

WARREN: But she has a problem: she can't read.

LAURA: What do you mean?

WARREN: She can comprehend phrases here and there. CeCe knows enough to check the right box. I look over her work before she turns it in. But she is – for all practical and professional purposes – occupationally illiterate.

LAURA: Is she a teenager?

WARREN: 27. With two kids. She was working fast food jobs before she got laid off and you don't need to be able to read to do that: just look at the pictures on the buttons and hit it.

LAURA: Wow...how does someone like that live?

WARREN: She lives like many people in these parts: poorly and in fear.

LAURA: "Fear is the cheapest room in the house."

WARREN: What?

LAURA: Rumi.

WARREN: No, whiskey.

LAURA: Corny.

WARREN: And it was Hafiz who said that, not Rumi.

LAURA: You're a smart ass.

WARREN: Look, after the campaign I figured we could help her out and get her into some adult education –

LAURA: – Warren, I don't think *we* can do that.

WARREN: Of course we can. We can do anything, remember? 'Yes, we can.' We're reaching out into the community. They show up for us, we can show up for them.

LAURA: Are you going to stay here and personally guide her education?

WARREN: Hell no. I'm going back to New York. But you're staying here? Getting a huge promotion in the party.

LAURA: It's not guaranteed. Warren, I've worked really hard to get this far in my career. And I just can't go around spending my political capital on people I don't know.

WARREN: But you're going to have more power.

LAURA: And responsibility.

WARREN: To the people.

LAURA: No, to the party.

WARREN: Laura, we can't just pick up and leave these people in the dark.

LAURA: That's politics.

WARREN: That's politics? Huh. I get it. This is why people hate us. This is why they slam the door in our faces, cuss and scream at us. We're just an occupying army squatting in their city.

LAURA: Don't be so dramatic.

WARREN: It has to be different. This time it's different.

LAURA: Why?

WARREN: Because that's what this campaign is all about, Laura. Isn't it? You were the one who wanted me to reach out to the people. Right?

LAURA: Warren…

WARREN: Right? Laura, what is wrong with you tonight?

Beat.

LAURA: I've got to take a leak.

WARREN: Such a lady.

LAURA exits. WARREN drains his drink. SAM enters and motions for another round.

WARREN: Sam!

SAM: Hey, Warren? What are you doing here?

WARREN: Mapping out my world conquest. You?

SAM: Just having a drink.

WARREN: Well join us. Laura is here.

SAM: Laura? You mean she decided to go out after she got the news?

WARREN: News?

SAM: You didn't hear? One of her relatives over in Iraq was in a major skirmish outside of Baghdad. They haven't heard from them in two days. Army isn't saying anything. She was on the phone and checking her email all afternoon trying to get answers.

WARREN: I guess she's good at holding it all in.

SAM: Sorry, maybe I shouldn't have said anything.

WARREN: Huh, well what do you know? You think you're getting to know someone and then it turns out you know nothing about them. They have an entire alternate reality underneath the surface.

SAM: You usually get this philosophical when you're drunk.

WARREN: I'm not drunk. Yet. Well...stick around for a drink. Pull up a stool, fool.

SAM: Actually I think I should be getting back to my table. But it was nice seeing you, man...

BARBARA: *(Entering.)* Sammy, what's the traffic jam with the drinks?

WARREN: Barbara? I thought you said you were having a drink with your husband?

BARBARA: I am.

Beat.

WARREN: Wait a minute...

SAM: Yes.

WARREN: Oh wow. Sammy! You think you know someone...

SAM: And then they got a whole other world going on.

WARREN: Sammy Sam Sam.

BARBARA: Only his wife gets to call him that.

WARREN: So you two kept your last names and are going marital incognito.

SAM: We got married a few months ago. In the middle of the campaign.

WARREN: Congratulations! Did you throw a party?!
If not, I can –

BARBARA: No, no, no! We prefer not to announce it.

WARREN: Why not?

SAM: It's not a big deal. But some gray-haired party types have very old-fashioned views and it can be viewed as un-professional and –

WARREN: – Oh, yes! Office incest. Yeah, I get it. We were told not to do that. Congrats. Does Laura know? *(They look at him.)* She doesn't. Well this is one big family affair.

BARBARA: If you could be so kind as to not blab this out to everyone…

WARREN: Sure sure Sammy! Wink wink, nudge nudge. Poke poke. The ol' ball and chain.

BARBARA: Oh God, if this is going to become some sort of boy's club I'm out of here.

SAM: I'll bring the drinks to the table, dear.

WARREN: No, no dear. You guys stay. We'll take off.

BARBARA: Who is 'we?'

WARREN: I'm here with Laura.

BARBARA: Great, half of Cleveland will know by tomorrow.

WARREN: No problem. I'll distract her and skillfully escort her out of the bar. We'll sober up at a diner and then I will drive her home.

SAM: You'd do that for us? It would make things a lot easier.

WARREN: *(Exiting.)* Of course. Just for you: Sammy. Babs. Bammy. Enjoy your drinks and you can pay me back for this later. See you two lovebirds tomorrow.

BARBARA: You know he's going to be an obnoxious jerk about this until the end of the campaign.

SAM: And this is where my skill as a peacemaker comes in. I will handle it.

BARBARA: Promise?

SAM: For you.

SAM and BARBARA kiss.

SCENE NINE: MOMENT OF TRUTH

INSTRUCTOR #2: Car. On the first morning of early voting your job on the front lines of early voting is to deliver coffee, water, and snacks. Volunteers, we are encouraging and lifting spirits.

WARREN drives CECE to polling station.

WARREN: What if they don't show up?

CECE: We knocked on every door.

WARREN: We have a high flake rate. People promise things and then never show up. They don't show up to do phone bank, they don't show up to volunteer, they just flake out. They look you dead in your face, smile, and then disappear. What if it's just us and a handful of people?

CECE: Why are you so nervous?

WARREN: The first day of early voting sets the tone for the rest of the campaign. If people aren't passionate and they stay home, then...what if they're right? Maybe I am just a stuck-up sell out. And the whole time they're laughing at me. And I can't get anyone to believe in anything I say.

CECE: I thought you said you can't take things personally.

WARREN: I lied. It's all personal. Every door slam, every time I was called 'nigger' on one side of the street and a 'sell-out' on the other, every cuss word hurled at me. One more red light to go... *(To CECE.)* Take my hand.

CECE: Why? What are we doing?

WARREN: Praying.

CECE: I thought you weren't into that.

WARREN: CeCe, I'm desperate. Go ahead and say something.

CECE: I can't speak well like you or like those ministers on TV.

WARREN: It's God. Just talk to Him like your sons.

CECE: Ok. God... I want you to be proud of me. I never done much with what you gave me. I was told my whole life that all I did was get in the way. Sometimes I feel like I wasn't supposed to be here. Like you made a mistake. But this is the first time I actually don't feel like I'm taking up space. And I met other people like me. And then I didn't feel so used up. I don't really know if our guy is gonna win or not, but please... I just don't want to be taking up space anymore. I want to make my sons, my mom, someone out there... I want to make someone proud. Like I was worth something. Amen.

WARREN: Amen. You've...thought those things before?

CECE: Every day, Mr. Warren. The light is green.

WARREN: Well...here goes nothing. You're going to have to tell me what you see. It's on your side.

CECE: I don't see anything yet.

WARREN: The sun is in my face. I can't see anything on my side either.

CECE: I think I can make out the building.

WARREN: And? And?!?!

CECE: Look at that.

WARREN: Look at what, CeCe?

CECE points and drags her finger across the horizon.

CECE: It goes all the way out the door, past the trees. Past the gates. And then the line wraps around. And around. And around. Looks like every single person in East Cleveland. Every different color, height, shape. Got men in suits and women in their pajamas, babies. Look at that. Can you pull over so I can take a picture, Mr. Clayton?

WARREN pulls over and they get out. CECE takes out her disposable camera and snaps a few pictures.

CECE: Well guess it's time to start handing out the supplies.

INSTRUCTOR #2: You are there to lift their spirits.

WARREN: But they were already a mile high. What is that song?

CECE: I used to sing that in the choir.

INSTRUCTOR #2: Gospel. Hymnals, spirituals. 'We Shall Overcome.' And…

CECE: *(Singing through the day.)*
Why should I feel discouraged?
And why should the shadows come?
Lord, why should my heart feel lonely?
And long for my heaven and home?

When Jesus is my portion.
A constant friend is He.
His eye is on the sparrow.
And I know, He watches over me.

I sing because I'm happy.
I sing because I'm free.
His eye is on the sparrow.
And I know He watches over me.

WARREN: What a day. I don't know what hurts more.

CECE: My feet ache and my shoulders got knives in them.

WARREN: But how do you feel?

CECE: I feel great. You?

WARREN: I feel like I finally know why I'm here.

CECE: Why's that?

WARREN: My father. It was always personal. Your sons.
My Dad.

CECE: Too bad the campaign is going to be over soon.

WARREN: Yes, but I want you to know that I'm not going to
leave you behind.

CECE: Leave me behind? Mr. Warren, what are you talking
about?

WARREN: I'm going to find you a good job training program
and some adult literacy courses. And you're going to make
your sons proud.

CECE: Mr. Warren, I don't need your pity.

WARREN: It's not pity. It's what friends do.

CECE: Oh, and I'm your friend now?

WARREN: Yes.

CECE: I don't have any friends, Mr. Warren.

WARREN: CeCe, I just want to help you.

CECE: Did I ask you to help me?

WARREN: Well…no but –

CECE: – no one asked for your help.

WARREN: But you need help! You need to learn how to read
and write.

CECE: I can read and write.

WARREN: Yeah, but not well. Not when we first met.

CECE: That's cause you were pressuring me. It made me nervous.

WARREN: I was standing in front of you with a pen and pad and asking you to sign it.

CECE: I don't know what you would have had me signing.

WARREN: That's why I wanted you to READ IT. And then what about the phone script? You didn't want to read that either. Did I make you nervous in that situation too?

CECE: Fuck this bullshit. Just drive me home.

WARREN: CeCe, if someone standing in front of you is too much pressure for you to gather yourself in order to read and sign a piece of paper, then that is a pretty clear indicator of poor literacy skills.

CECE: Negro, who made you the judge of what's poor and what's not?

WARREN: I know what you need.

CECE: Oh, you do?

WARREN: You need basic education. You need to be functionally literate. I don't know what schools you went to, but you should not be a 27-year-old woman incapable of signing your name under mild duress. That is not acceptable. It hurts my guts to see you like that.

CECE: I'm sorry if I'm such a pathetic piece of shit that I upset your stomach.

WARREN: CeCe, that's not what I meant –

CECE: I'm done. You know, I see people like you every once and awhile. You come into my hood, trying to get my vote, or get me to sign a petition. Knocking on my doors. Do-good niggas. And you smile and look at me like I'm a fucking 3-legged dog or one of those Africans babies on the TV with flies buzzing around their eyes. You get it in your head that I need your help. But once you get what you need, your heart stops hurting, and you just disappear. All that charity dries up the second you get what you want. No, sir. I've had my fill of do-good niggas. But you know what, I'm done. I don't need your welfare or your help. You can go back to your city and I'll stay in mine. You can save your pity and do-good's.

WARREN: CECE. CECE!!!

INSTRUCTOR #2: Campaigns can be very emotional. At times it may feel overwhelming.

WARREN: I can't believe this. What am I going to do?

INSTRUCTOR #2: And when those times come, just look around and call for help.

Beat.

INSTRUCTOR #2: *(Exiting.)* Well go on.

WARREN looks around and finds that he's all alone.

WARREN: HEEEEEEELLLLLLP!!!!!!

BLACK OUT

END OF ACT ONE

ACT TWO

SCENE ONE: FINAL STRETCH

INSTRUCTOR #1: In the last few weeks, you get the bandwagon riders, latecomers, and campaign tourists parading through with their cameras who spend more time snapping pictures of themselves than working. East Coasters: the final wave of New Yorkers, Jersey-ites, and Bostonians. Volunteers, you must remain patient.

WARREN: Maybe she'll show up today.

INSTRUCTOR #1: Forget about her and don't linger on the past. Remember: cool, calm, and –

WARREN: – Keep it moving, I know.

Office of volunteers appear. LAINEY and BRAD, pose for pictures by Black people. CAITS, a Black New Jersey woman in her 20s, stands next to them.

WARREN: Thank you guys so much for joining us in the home stretch of GOTV. We are 'getting out the vote' and are really –

LAINEY: Can I get a picture? It's for Facebook. Brad?

LAINEY poses next to WARREN in a variety of gangsta and hip hop poses that's mildly offensive. BRAD snaps away on his phone.

BRAD: Work it, work it, look at my baby work it!

WARREN: Where are you guys from?

BRAD: Tribeca.

WARREN: New York. Me too.

BRAD: Oh, I thought you said you were from Brooklyn?

WARREN: Anyway, we are really excited to have all you newbies. You have been trained and we'll partner you up in teams. Why don't you introduce yourself…

BRAD: I'm Brad Obama. And this is my baby….

LAINEY: Lainey Obama. We decided to adopt Obama's name in the last month as a sign of solidarity. I just think it's so amazing how far we've come as a country when it comes to race. It's like we're wiping the slate clean and we're not Blacks or Whites. We're just Americans. Get on board everybody! Post-racial America is set to leave the station!

WARREN: There is so much I want to say to you right now, Lainey and Brad. Yeah, so much to say but just *(Fighting urge.)* …thank you. Your help is appreciated and needed.

LAINEY: You're welcome, brotha.

WARREN: So much I want to say. And you, young lady?

CAITS: What about me?

BRAD: What's your name, sister?

CAITS: Caits.

LAINEY: Where are you from, Caits?

CAITS: I'm from the People's Republic of Mind Your Own Damn Business.

WARREN: All right, this is where I step in and say that this is a very intense time. But all of us will grow closer together.

LAINEY: Absolutely. This is post-racial America –

WARREN: – Stop saying that. Now, we're going to split people up into teams to scour the area. Normally we would do one or two people. But since everyone here is new, I figured the three of you can go together. Get to know each other.

BRAD: Warren, brother…can I talk to you for a second? *(To WARREN.)* Listen, I don't think it's such a good idea to have that pairing. I'm sensing some hostility from Caits.

WARREN: Brad, I know you guys traveled all the way from the great city of Tribeca for this. And I appreciate that. So why not give peace a chance?

BRAD: We didn't sign up to get some guilt trip from Sista Souljah.

WARREN: Look I'm not going to force anyone on you. You guys can go out with Barbara when she gets back okay?

BRAD: Barbara isn't angry, is she?

WARREN: On second thought, when Sam gets back you can go out with him. I'll pair up with Caits. But you and Caits should still talk at some point in time. I'm sure she's just as nervous as all the rest of us.

BRAD gives a 'thug pound' gesture of solidarity to WARREN and exits. LIGHT SHIFT to CAITS and WARREN.

CAITS: Why you kissing them white folks' asses?

WARREN: I'm not kissing their ass, Caits. We were talking. Now here is the area we're working –

CAITS: – But you in charge so why didn't you just tell them off?

WARREN: Being in charge doesn't mean being a bully. It's about getting the work done…partner.

CAITS: Whatever.

WARREN: Caits, I do require all my partners to answer one question: why are you here?

CAITS: – My brother.

WARREN: Oh, how sweet. How old is he?

CAITS: I thought you only said one question.

INSTRUCTOR #2: When a new volunteer is approaching someone on the street, make sure they're not too nervous or scared.

WARREN: Now when you go up to someone on the street try to –

CAITS: Hey! HEEEY!! Yeah you? You voting for Obama or what? You're not sure. What the hell –

WARREN: – Caits, a little less police interrogation.

INSTRUCTOR #2: If you run across a rough area, use your judgment skills to help out newcomers and steer them clear of trouble.

WARREN: Now let's skip this area. Some rougher types so –

CAITS: AY-YOOO!!! Nigga, you ain't voted yet? Take your Black ass down there. Job? It's 1 p.m. in the afternoon. You ain't got no job!

INSTRUCTOR #2: After a long day in the field, it's important to have those quiet moments at night with your partner.

CAITS looks up.

WARREN: Caits? Ay-yo, Caits?!!

CAITS: Damn, man! Can't a sista get a moment of silence?

WARREN: I'm trying out my slang…yo. I'm slingin' slang and doing my thang. How does it sound?

CAITS: Corny. Like you.

WARREN: Why are staring at the street lights?

CAITS: None of your damn business.

WARREN: Hey Caits, I'm just trying to relate to –

CAITS: – Forget it! You ain't never gonna relate, partner!! Okay? You ain't never going to relate cause you phony, weak, and trifling. Now let's just get on with the work.

WARREN walks away from her.

CAITS: What are you doing?

WARREN: I need a break.

CAITS: Yo, Warren. You can't be taking everything I say so seriously dude. I was just…

WARREN: *(Exiting.)* I need to go talk to a friend.

CAITS: You ain't got no friends, man. What happened to 'cool, calm, and keep it moving.' Man, forget you nigga!

SCENE TWO: LA DOLCE VITA

INSTRUCTOR #2: Dear volunteers, it's important to move forward through turbulent emotions.

WARREN stands outside CECE's door and knocks.

WARREN: CeCe? I know you're home. Celeste Robinson. Come on! Open up!

INSTRUCTOR #2: Don't linger on those who have flaked out.

WARREN: So what am I supposed to do? Just leave them behind?

INSTRUCTOR #2: Yes.

WARREN: No. I reject that advice. CeCe, come out and talk!!!

INSTRUCTOR #2: Why?

WARREN: I reject that advice because it makes me feel miserable.

INSTRUCTOR #2: This campaign is bigger than you, Warren. It's bigger than your feelings. You don't want to become like your predecessor, Phil.

WARREN: I finally inspired someone and they quit like that. I just don't understand it.

INSTRUCTOR #2: – Remember, you are the face of the campaign: cool. Calm.

WARREN: I don't give a fuck! And I will not remain calm!

INSTRUCTOR #2: Dear volunteer, having a public meltdown may attract attention. It may draw a crowd. People from around the neighborhood. Do not become like a Phil. Do not make yourself the object of –

WARREN: – Oh, I'm sorry America. Did I attract attention? Did I disturb you? Did I interrupt your lovely lives of smoking, fucking, and deep-frying yourself to death?!? As you rot from the inside, as your brains ooze like so much liquid cheese that you consume, who am I to try to stop you? Your homes are in foreclosed ruins. We just gave a trillion dollars of *your* tax money to the same con artist who drained your workers' pension plans and liquidated your factories. Your high school graduates can't read above the level of a comic book, your children have diabetes before they lose their baby teeth, and every two years we struggle to get just half of you guys to waddle your fat asses down to a polling booth and push a button. Like voting is the biggest inconvenience that could be imposed upon your busy schedule of posting cat videos on YouTube and stealing your grandmother's prescription pills from her purse. You have lost everything important and you don't even know it because you have been bamboozled by 400 channels of nothing, phone apps, gladiator blood sports, and "The Real Housewives of Wherever-the-fuck-!" And most of them aren't even real housewives! They're just girlfriends and baby mamas!! But am I sorry for waking you up, America. Please slip back into your coma. I wouldn't want to stop the rancid terminal decay that is otherwise known as "LA DOLCE FUCKING VITA!"

WARREN collapses onto the steps of the house. NEIGHBOR walks up smoking a cigarette.

NEIGHBOR: La Doggy who?

WARREN: …what?

NEIGHBOR: You said La Doggy fucking what?

WARREN: I said La Dolce Vita –

NEIGHBOR: – Yeah, yeah, what's that?

WARREN: It means 'the sweet life,' in Italian. It's also a movie.

NEIGHBOR: So there's a movie out there called "La Dolce Fucking Vita?"

WARREN: No, I added the 'fucking.' I was being sarcastic. And I'm sorry. That was completely unprofessional.

NEIGHBOR: You mean to tell me that someone hired you for a profession?

WARREN: The Obama campaign.

NEIGHBOR: That's where I seen you from. Marching up and down these here streets.

WARREN: Yes ma'am. Listen, I'm sorry if I disturbed you.

NEIGHBOR: No, not at all. I was just fixing to head off to bed when my husband told me there was some herky-jerky looking thing standing outside. And so he called the cops –

WARREN: The cops!!

NEIGHBOR: Yeah, but don't worry. They ain't gonna be here for at least a few hours so you got time to relax. Last week we called to report someone busting into a house that had been padlocked. Don't you know this burglar had time to raid the fridge, cook an omelette, watched an episode of *American Idol*, and re-tile the kitchen before the first patrol car rolled by. I supposed it was for the best cause the person breaking into the house was the homeowner's cousin just trying to grab some of his clothes before the bank came by and threw it all away. So since the cops are gonna take a while, I figured I would go see what the herking and jerking was about.

WARREN: I was trying to talk to Celeste Robinson.

NEIGHBOR: CeCe not home. What did you want to talk to her about?

WARREN: Ummm…voting. Look, I should be –

NEIGHBOR: – Oh yes. I'm going down after church to get my ballot.

WARREN: Are you voting for Obama?

NEIGHBOR: No, I'm voting for the other Black man on the ballot: Count Chocula. Of course I'm voting for Barack Obama!

WARREN: You bringing down some friends or family members with you?

NEIGHBOR: No, chile. Just my husband. All my friends and family are gone. I'm all that's left.

WARREN: Oh, sorry. Well hey, you're carrying on the legacy.

NEIGHBOR: I guess. I tell you one thing though: he better win.

WARREN: Why?

NEIGHBOR: If this man don't win, then that would…hurt. It would hurt my feelings, hurt my soul. It would just hurt all over. I would be done. And I think a lot of other people would be too.

WARREN: Then why is this so difficult?

NEIGHBOR: Difficult? This is easy. I couldn't vote when I was your age. And then when it was technically legal they made all the Blacks in my town take some ridiculous poll test. The kind of test with impossible questions like name all the state capitals, list all the bill of rights, and recite the entire Declaration of Independence from front to back. Trying to stop me.

WARREN: I can't believe people would deny you that.

NEIGHBOR: Oh, they didn't deny me nothing.

WARREN: But I thought you said they made you take that insane test –

NEIGHBOR: "When in the Course of human events, it becomes necessary for one people to dissolve the political bands which have connected them with another, and to assume among the powers of the earth, the separate and equal station to which the Laws of Nature and of Nature's God entitle them, a decent respect to the opinions of mankind requires that they should declare the causes which impel them to the separation. We hold these truths to be self-evident, that all men are created equal, that they are endowed by their Creator with certain unalienable Rights, that among these are Life, Liberty and the pursuit of Happiness." Shall I continue or do you want me to move on to the state capitals?

WARREN: That was...

NEIGHBOR: That was just what had to be done. So that you could stand here today ranting about how hard everything is.

WARREN: Sorry about that. I just don't know if I can do this.

NEIGHBOR: You can and you will. We all will. What other choice do we have?

WARREN: Quit.

NEIGHBOR: And then you lose everything.

WARREN: But I'm tired of following all these instructions and rules.

NEIGHBOR: See, right there is your problem. Who told you, you had to follow all the rules?

WARREN: But the campaign organizers...

NEIGHBOR: Lord help me with this fool. You went to college right?

WARREN: Yes.

NEIGHBOR: Yeah, I could tell. And yet you don't know nothing. "Any fool who follows all the rules ends up just another broken tool." You improvise, baby. Didn't that college teach you that? Course not, why would they teach you something you can use in life when you're paying them $100,000. Most rules are just advices. And most advice is just a suggestion. You take a suggestion and you bend it like taffy. It ain't the 10 commandments. They're not going to crack. Lightning isn't going to strike you dead.

> The only thing you're going to learn from improvising is what kind of man you are.

WARREN: 'The man I am.' I would like to know that.

NEIGHBOR: Then you better get started.

WARREN: You're right. I should be going. I got another long evening ahead of me.

NEIGHBOR: That sounds like a complaint.

WARREN: It's just a weary observation.

NEIGHBOR: Get yourself some coffee.

WARREN: Will do, ma'am. I'll see you later?

NEIGHBOR: On Sunday, down at the polling station.

WARREN: Sounds good. Now to go pick up some double-shot espresso.

NEIGHBOR: Just remember this: you will never be as tired as your ancestors.

WARREN: I know. La Dolce Vita.

SCENE THREE: 3 AM PRAYERS

WARREN is driving CAITS home.

INSTRUCTOR #3: The streets. Night. At the end of the workday you are faced with that long ride home through the darkened streets of your territory. And in that quiet journey there is a sort of calm tranquility that makes you believe that if cities could pray, then late nights like these would be their hour of reverential worship.

CAITS: I can't believe it's almost 3 a.m. You guys work this hard every day?

WARREN: Seven days a week. And then we get up in a few hours and do it all over again. You're lucky that you came in at the end, Caits. Saved yourself a lot of gray hairs.

CAITS: *(Looking in mirror.)* There's a car that's following us.

WARREN: I know. It's a cop. It was in the campaign office parking lot.

INSTRUCTOR #3: Dear volunteer, when you are being followed at 3 a.m. by police officers, be sure to lower your speed, use turn signals, stay within the lines of the road. Take all necessary precautions.

CAITS: Fuck, I hate cops!

WARREN: Well… I don't know about 'hate' –

CAITS: I FUCKING HATE COPS!

INSTRUCTOR #3: If you have a passenger in the car with you and they appear agitated, try to calm them down.

WARREN: Okkkaaay! Those are some strong feelings there, Caits. Why do you hate cops so much?

CAITS: Nevermind. Why are they following us?

INSTRUCTOR #3: Remind them that they are the face of the campaign.

WARREN: Just be Obama: cool and calm.

WARREN looks through mirror while he talks. They engage in tense small-talk.

WARREN: So, Caits is that a Long Island accent?

CAITS: Nah, man. Patterson, New Jersey. Pig is still following us. Why doesn't he just pull us over?

WARREN: Don't know. You said before that you have a brother?

CAITS: Had a brother. But he was killed.

WARREN: Sorry to hear that. Umm…

CAITS: He was killed in a traffic stop.

INSTRUCTOR #3: When dealing with those horrific moments of cosmic irony, try to change the subject as quickly as possible.

WARREN: Caits, do you believe in God?

CAITS: Hell no!

WARREN: Great. I got something you might like: Buddhism.

CAITS: Oh like that Tina Turner 'nom, yo ho ren ge kuo' shit?

WARREN: Well. No. I mean that's one type but I practice something called –

Police lights and sirens start.

CAITS: Shit.

WARREN: To be continued.

CAITS: Why aren't you pulling over?

INSTRUCTOR #3: Be sure to pull into a well-lit area. Repeat pull into a well-lit area. Do not give them any reason to shoot you.

WARREN: Wouldn't want an accidental 'flash' of something to be mistaken by a nervous cop.

CAITS: Why the hell would he be nervous? He's the one with a gun.

WARREN: Yes, but he's by himself. It's 3 a.m. and he's pulling over two people whom he doesn't know from Adam. Up ahead is a well-lit…

INSTRUCTOR #3: …major intersection. Pull up there. Take your wallet out of your pocket. Now place both hands on the steering wheel. Be sure to fully extend and lock the elbows.

WARREN: Yeah, we're Black. We are aware of the procedure.

WARREN and CAITS rigidly stick their arms out, like they're stretched on to the dashboard. NIGHT COP walks up in a rage.

NIGHT COP: Why didn't you pull over when I turned on my sirens?!?

INSTRUCTOR #3: Stare straight ahead. Do not look down at your lap or give any sudden movements. If they try to incite you, just stare straight ahead.

WARREN: I couldn't see anything, officer.

NIGHT COP: WELL YOU STOP WHEN I TELL YOU TO!

CAITS: Officer, is there a reason why we're getting pulled over?

INSTRUCTOR #3: Calm any agitated passengers.

WARREN: Caits, would you be so kind as to shut the fuck up. *(To COP.)* Here is my license –

WARREN drops his wallet on the ground and as he reaches down, NIGHT COP puts his hand on his holster. Suddenly, time stands still.

INSTRUCTOR #3: From this position, there are numerous fatal passageways a bullet can take from an officer's gun to a seated driver. The arteries in the neck, through the shoulder, down through the chest, or directly into your head.

Time unfreezes. CAITS screams.

WARREN: CAITS!!!

CAITS stops screaming. NIGHT COP takes his hand off the holster. He grabs WARREN's license and exits.

WARREN: Giving, morality, patience, effort, concentration, and wisdom.

CAITS: What?

WARREN: That's my spiritual practice. It's called the 6 perfections.

CAITS: What the hell does that have to do with anything?

WARREN: When you're in a difficult situation, you're supposed to practice the 6 perfections. Giving: handing over my license. Morality: following the law. Patience: not getting angry. Effort: exerting mental energy to stay calm. Concentration: meditating on one thing.

CAITS: And what's that?

WARREN: Going home. I want to go home. You want to go home. So let's do what we have to, and make sure everyone goes home. And wisdom: your brother.

CAITS: What the fuck do you know about my brother? Huh? He was handicapped, had learning disabilities, and was still working two jobs. Never complained, always busted his ass. He planned on going back to school. He wasn't just some piece of shit junkie like Rodney King. He was somebody. And the cops who did it? Two months of paid leave. They beat him until he stopped breathing...and got a vacation. So what the fuck would you know about that?

WARREN: You're going to learn from him. And then you're going to teach me. That's the wisdom. You're going to teach me how to remain calm. How to learn to play this game so that we can get home.

CAITS: What if he arrests us? Or worse?

WARREN: I can't control that. So let's just sit here. And meditate.

CAITS: You're really...really weird.

WARREN: Tell me something I don't know.

Beat.

CAITS: Every night when I look up at the street lights... I think of him. And that traffic stop.

WARREN: And so we sat there looking up at the street lights. In meditative silence on an East Cleveland back road at 3 am.

I thought about Caits' brother. And the Cleveland police. And even the cop right here with us. He was by himself, couldn't have been older than 25 or 26. He probably had a young wife or girlfriend. And he most definitely did not want to be out here with us. He wanted to go home. And if prayers do matter, then this should have three times as much power. Because we all wanted the same thing. But were too scared and too proud to say it.

NIGHT COP walks back to car. His demeanor is completely transformed.

NIGHT COP: Here you go, Mr. Clayton. Could you hit that switch right there?

WARREN fiddles with dial.

NIGHT COP: Now the other way. There you go. You had your dimmers on.

WARREN: That's it?

NIGHT COP: Not unless you want to confess something.

WARREN: Oh. Well…thank you.

CAITS: You followed us out of the parking lot before we even hit the road because OUR LIGHTS WERE DIM?!?

WARREN: CAITS!!

CAITS: Fine. I'm shutting up.

NIGHT COP: Go home. And have a good night.

CAITS: Yeah.

WARREN: Have a good night, officer.

They watch as the NIGHT COP walks away. They wait until he's out of sight before breaking into a jubilant slap-dance of freedom.

CAITS: That was amazing. It's like he came to our car as this Robocop asshole. And then he came back as a completely different person.

WARREN: Then that just proves he was never actually that Robocop asshole to begin with.

CAITS: What?

WARREN: Never mind: a long story. *(To INSTRUCTOR.)* I drove Caits home.

CAITS: Six perfections.

WARREN: Remember them.

CAITS tries elaborate handshake. WARREN fights her. CAITS gets out of the car and looks up at street light.

CAITS: Corey. His name was Corey. Remember that.

SCENE FOUR: CONVENIENCE STORE VICTORS

INSTRUCTOR #2: Convenience store. There is a ghostly silence that floats through a city after it's been bombarded with non-stop campaigning for 12 months. And now it's the final hours. The day before the final votes. It's just you and your shadow.

Store clerk is quietly weeping. She walks by WARREN completely ignoring him.

STORE CLERK: Can I help you?

WARREN: I'm fine, Janice. I –

STORE CLERK: Okay.

WARREN: *(Annoyed at first.)* Hey, Janice. Wait…are you crying? What's wrong?

STORE CLERK: I'm just a bit shook up. I mean…what is this country coming to? They're saying that man might win tomorrow. If he does then it's the end. Just you wait and see. We're all going to be Communists. We're going to be Obama-ists.

WARREN: I don't think that's in his platform.

JANICE cries. WARREN tries to comforts her. But he starts giggling.

JANICE: Why are you laughing?

WARREN: I don't know. I think I find your bigoted tears...
amusing.

JANICE: That's not very nice.

WARREN: I know, I know. I'm really trying to be
magnanimous. I am trying not to think about all the times
you followed me around in the store. All the times I've
been followed by people like you. All the times soon-to-be
president was followed by people like you out of suspicion.
But I can't help it. When I see you shed those bitter little
tears I can't help but laugh. Laugh like this...

WARREN lets out a huge, hearty, belting wave of chuckling.

JANICE: *(Exiting.)* You are cruel.

WARREN: Janice, wait! Don't go. Please follow me around the
store. Follow me to make sure I don't steal the detergent.
Follow me so I won't pocket some cashews. I need you to
follow me so I can laugh.

SAM enters with an envelope.

SAM: That wasn't very Buddha of you.

WARREN: I know but I've been sitting on that for a few
centuries. What are you doing here?

SAM: Just doing some friendly stalking. Well this is it.
Tomorrow is the day. It's all out of our hands now.
Did it meet your expectations?

WARREN: What?

SAM: The campaign.

WARREN: No.

SAM: Why?

WARREN: I guess I thought something that would change with
me.

SAM hands him an envelope.

WARREN: What is this?

SAM: Open it.

WARREN: Are these my numbers? *(SAM motions for him to open the envelope.)* Here comes more depressing news. *(Opens envelope and sees a spreadsheet of listings.)* Sam, what is this? These aren't my numbers.

SAM: Warren: have you thought about taking a position in the administration?

WARREN: What administration? We haven't won yet.

SAM: Yes, but if we pull this out there will be a lot of would-be low-level job opening. A great chance for someone like you to really take off.

WARREN: Sam… I'm still hung-over from last few all-nighters. And you want me to make a life-changing decision in a convenience store?

SAM: Yes. To the victors go the spoils and everyone is scrambling around for a spot.

BARBARA: *(Entering tired.)* Sam, what's the hold-up? I need some V-8.

SAM: Just ran into Warren who is having a pre-election day existential crisis.

WARREN: It's not a crisis. Just anxiety.

BARBARA: The empty-nest syndrome for campaigns. I get it all the time. And you know what the cure is?

WARREN: What?

BARBARA: The next election. The next job.

WARREN: But what about East Cleveland?

BARBARA: Forget it. This place is yesterday. In 24 hours it will feel like Siberia and it'll be about as political useful too.

WARREN: And what about the people here?

BARBARA: You'll forget them. And they'll forget you.

WARREN: So what do we leave behind?

SAM: Data and empty water bottles. So you're coming to DC with us?

BARBARA: Honey, did we discuss bringing Warren along?

SAM: Come on, he'll adapt. I can't believe you still hate him.

BARBARA: That is not the issue. Warren, I don't hate you.

WARREN: Thanks. Huh, I guess none of this mattered after all. I guess I was delusional to think that –

SAM: – you shut your freaking face… Warren.

BARBARA: Sammy?

SAM: I will not stand here listening to this pity party. I am… I am getting tough on you. You know what they are calling me around the office now? Hard Tit. Hard Tit cause I don't take no 'shit.' And this Hard Titty is getting tough on you, because you are not a delicate flower. And I won't coddle you or anyone else. Now you are going to take these papers because this is your future. And after all this work, I am not going to let you destroy that.

SAM shoves the envelope in WARREN's pocket.

SAM: Once tomorrow is here and you see the numbers up on the big board, you'll feel differently. But for now…toughen yourself.

Beat.

WARREN: Barbara, what was that?

BARBARA: Good try, honey. Listen, Warren you don't have to rush into any decision. Just sit back and look at what you did. Look at the history you help make.

SCENE FIVE: BALLROOM

INSTRUCTOR #3: *(Slightly drunk.)* Downtown Cleveland. Hilton Ballroom. Election night.

WARREN and SAM stand there holding their drinks. They are inebriated but not drunk.

INSTRUCTOR #3: Now volunteers, some of you may have begun your partying a bit early the past few days as all the campaign business wrapped up. So enjoy these complimentary drinks. In moderation. Remember, cool and calm. And keep it in moderation. If you need more drink tickets, see Laura or Barbara. Have fun and what are we?

WARREN/SAM: Fired up and ready to sleep!!! *(Fake snooze.)*

WARREN: Look: the hordes of malnourished, sleep deprived staffers are attacking the free bar. This is not going to end well.

SAM: Oh, first person to vomit. Ooo-pa!

WARREN: Ooo-pa!

Beat.

WARREN: Well?

SAM: Well…what should we talk about?

INSTRUCTOR #3: Exchange war stories.

SAM: Remember when that old lady had her dog chase you across her yard?

WARREN: Remember when we almost had a gun pulled on us?

SAM: Remember when that guy threatened to kill me?

WARREN: Remember when your wife thought I was going to fuck everything up?

SAM: Good times.

SAM: Well I always knew you could do it.

WARREN: No, you didn't.

SAM: You're right. You were quite awful for a while.
The turning point was that woman you brought in
who got her whole block out.

WARREN: Yeah, CeCe.

SAM: Is she 'tardy for the party?'

WARREN: M.I.A.

SAM: I wonder what happened to her?

WARREN: I don't know. Sam, I was wondering if you could
pull some strings for CeCe. Get her into a job training
program and adult literacy classes.

SAM: That's not my field of expertise.

WARREN: Come on, just one more job.

SAM: No.

WARREN: Damn, Sam! People in the office used to think you
were softer than baby's feet. But you've changed, man.
And you have earned your new nickname cause you are
one hard-titty'ed bitch. That's a name that might stick.

SAM: I would welcome a change after being called 'cracker'
and 'cracker-ass-cracker' and 'motherfucking bitch-ass-
cracker' and my all time favorite of 'lemur-with-loose-
cookie-monster-eyes-white-devil-bitch-ass-nutty-cracker.'
And after being called all these things and more for several
months, the rustic charm of East Cleveland has worn off.
I have reached my limit. And it hasn't been easy.

WARREN: Well neither was hiding your marriage.
That certainly wasn't easy. But I did it. From the office-
incest allegations to protect you.

SAM: And here I thought you were going to let me escape Cleveland without playing that card.

WARREN: Listen Hard Tit, you and Barbara owe me. It's time to pay up.

SAM: I have no power here. You gotta talk to Laura.

WARREN: You guys can lean on her. We have to start doing things differently.

LAURA: *(Entering.)* Look: the numbers are coming in for the first state. This is it!

WARREN: Laura, how are you?

LAURA: Hanging in there.

WARREN: What about your sister?

LAURA: Germany.

WARREN: How did she end up in Germany?

LAURA: Hospital. It's where they take soldiers who have more serious injuries. But I'll think about all that later.

WARREN: Okay, well my thoughts are with you…

LAURA: Thank you very much.

WARREN: And if you need anything –

LAURA: – Warren. I've come this far white knuckling this and biting my lips so I'll manage. And if I talk about this anymore right now, I will have a mental breakdown. Okay?

WARREN: Okay.

LAURA: Thank you. Besides, you should be celebrating. We should all be…having a good time and getting ready for the final numbers.

WARREN: State by state the data poured in and the map lit up blue and red. As we approached that quantum moment, that historical point of reckoning, there she was.

CECE enters.

SAM: Well look who decided to make an appearance.

CECE: Celeste Robinson. My friends call me CeCe.

SAM: Yes, I know you. I'm –

WARREN: – Hard-Titty.

SAM: Sam. You and Warren did great work together. The office wasn't the same after you left.

CECE: I'm sure Warren and you managed to hold things together.

WARREN: So CeCe, you came down to see history?

CECE: No. I came to see you.

SAM: Maybe I should leave you two alone –

WARREN: No, it's not like that. Unlike you, some people can separate the personal and professional.

CECE: But I would like to talk to you alone for a minute.

SAM exits.

CECE: I just wanted to say to you…that you had no right to come to my house banging on my door like that.

WARREN: I wanted to talk to you.

CECE: Why, so you could make me feel like shit again?

WARREN: That's not what I wanted to do. I just wanted to check in and make sure you were okay.

CECE: Oh. Well I was working. Got my old job back at McDonald's.

WARREN: McDonald's. You're happy with that?

CECE: It's work, Mr. Warren. It's not supposed to make me happy.

WARREN: Then congratulations. I wish you all the unhappiness that you seek.

CECE: What is your fucking problem?

WARREN: I know you don't want to be working there and you don't have to be. And I think it's important that you consider what you're giving to your kids: fear. Fear of failure. Fear of trying. Fear of having hope. And fear is hereditary. I know cause I have some of my parents' cowardice in me. I know because I run from that same fear all the time. And I know because I haven't talked to my parents in months because of that fear. But you don't have to pass that on. And you shouldn't deprive them of a better life.

LAURA: *(Running through.)* We just won Pennsylvania!!!!

CECE: I'm not depriving them of anything. And who are you to judge?

WARREN: Who am I? I just told you! I am you. I know what it's like to be a coward.

CECE: Are you calling me a coward?

WARREN: I am calling you out for your sons. How are they going to look at you when they get older? What are you going to tell them?

CECE: That I did this! That I actually did something important.

WARREN: And then they're going to ask 'why did you stop, Mom?' And then what are you going to say? That you were tired. That you could work hard for Obama but not for yourself? Or for them?

LAURA: VIRGINIA!!! Holy cow!!! We got Virginia!!!

CECE: I got a job that pays. So what am I supposed to do? Quit that for school? And then what? What if I can't do the homework, what if I can't pass the tests? What if I flunk out and it turns out that I'm as stupid as everyone thinks I am? Then what happens?

WARREN: I don't know, CeCe. But you gotta decide if you're going to be different. And it doesn't take brains or education to try. Just stand up. When a friend offers you help –

CECE: – you're not my friend, Warren. Don't you get that?!? Friends have to be equal. And we're not.

WARREN: No, we're not! We're not equals but that's because you don't want to be.

CECE: So it's my fault?

WARREN: I think it's comforting you. So you don't have to take any responsibility. If you're just a number, then you don't have to do the hard work. And this isn't the uppity Negro talking. This is the weary Black man who is tired of seeing my people take comfort in being statistics. We were brought here in chains. Numbers in a ship register. And now we're still numbers. Prisons. Drop-outs, murder, crime, drugs, unemployment. Single Black mothers. Numbers! I am tired of not seeing faces. And for a moment, you stepped out from behind those numbers. You were Celeste 'CeCe' Robinson from East Cleveland. Born and raised. Professional campaigner, community activist. Leader. Mother. And after all this...you're going to step back behind the veil of numbers. And what do you think your sons are going to be? A face or a stat line?

CECE: So that's it, huh? You've made your judgment on me and all the numbers out here in the world? It must feel great to be so right about everyone.

WARREN: CeCe, this isn't about being right. It's about doing better.

CECE: And what are you doing to make things better?

WARREN: Trying to help you.

CECE: I'm talking about for you, Mr. Warren. Not me. You. How can you help me when you can't even help yourself? You can't even get over your own shit.

WARREN: But...

CECE: It must be great to know what everyone else needs to do except you, Warren.

WARREN starts to walk away.

CECE: So you're going to run away? Isn't that what you said you've been doing your whole life? I thought you said this was different.

WARREN pauses for a moment and then exits.

LAURA: WE GOT OHIO!!! We did it!!

There is a final eruption of celebration and cheers. And then it all fades away.

SCENE SIX: THE MAN I AM

Doorway. WARREN stands in the darkness of the street for a moment.

INSTRUCTOR #3: The post-campaign crash comes hard, dear volunteer. People forget awfully quick. The next day the headquarters were deserted. Within 72 hours all the furniture, phones, and supplies had vanished. Like you were never there. And then you're left with you again. And that ache.

WARREN knocks on the door.

INSTRUCTOR #3: For old time sakes you might find yourself longing for a door to knock on, a person to introduce yourself to, a stranger to believe in you.

WARREN's MOM opens the door. Holiday decorations and warm lighting floods the doorway. She stands there looking at him.

WARREN: Mom. Hi, how are you doing?

MOM stares at him.

WARREN: I'm fine. Thanks for asking. I bet you and Dad were up late on election night. The whole world was celebrating. I don't know where it's going to go or if it's even going to work but...it's a movement. I did that, Mom. Your son.

MOM looks at him suspiciously.

WARREN: I just wanted to stop by and say that to you and Dad. If he's around I could say talk to him too.

MOM begins to move back into the house.

WARREN: Or not. Listen...wait.

MOM stops.

WARREN: It's just me. I'm not a vampire. But I have been a coward. Running away from you guys, from my friends. Running away from who I am. I know you're not happy about some of the decisions I've made, but I hope you guys can appreciate this one: no more running. No more hiding. So I am standing here today without apologies. And if you can accept that...and me...then I want to try to be a family. If you can't accept that...

WARREN begins to back away, but he's hoping that she will stop him. MOM begins to soften.

WARREN: And if you can't accept me, then I will leave you guys alone.

MOM turns around and looks at a person down the hallway. DAD is heard off-stage.

DAD *(O/S.)*: Joanne, you're letting all the heat out. Who's at the door?

Beat.

DAD *(O/S.)*: Come on, who is it?

MOM slowly closes the door in his face. WARREN is back in darkness of the street.

INSTRUCTOR #3: Like I said, for the sake of old times you might find yourself longing for a door to knock on, a person to introduce yourself to, or a stranger to believe in you.

SCENE SEVEN: HAFIZ

WARREN: Back in New York, there were many email blasts. All the volunteers kept vowing to meet up again. And I missed the first gathering. For the second meeting, I was out of town. And it all just trickled away. But I guess it was for the best. No nostalgic reminiscing. Sam and Barbara moved to D.C. I think it was to become staffers but the details are hazy now. And then an entire year passed without me thinking about Cleveland or anyone in the campaign. Then another year before I got an email. From CeCe.

CECE: I am sending you this message from the training center in downtown Cleveland.

WARREN: CeCe? It's been years. How are you doing?

CECE: I am writing. And no one is helping me…

WARREN: Well…congratulations.

CECE: Some workers from the campaign office got me connected to a few good people. And then they connected me to that White lady who ran the office.

WARREN: Laura?

CECE: Yes. And she said I might even be able to take a position in the party if I keep working. The local party. Nothing big, but maybe a secretary.

WARREN: That's still great.

CECE: And what about you?

WARREN: Still drifting a bit.

CECE: You need to get your ass back to Cleveland. You had purpose here.

WARREN: Our emails became texts. And then phone calls. And then another year passed and CeCe was hired. And then promoted. *(On phone.)* Laura is a good person to know. I'm glad she promoted you. She knows you'll work hard.

CECE: She had some help in the picking.

WARREN: Really?

CECE: Yes, Sam and Barbara.

WARREN: That's good. They finally left behind a mark.

CECE: And so did you. I'm surprised you're not Obama's chief of staff by now.

WARREN: Things don't always turn out like we expect them to.

CECE: Weren't you offered a position in the administration?

WARREN: It wasn't the right time.

CECE: If not now, then when?

WARREN: I don't know. Maybe his second term.

CECE: Second term? You're really confident in him.

WARREN: I'm confident in what was created that year. It'll carry Obama and then keep carrying on past him.

CECE: Well then if you don't want the White House chief of staff, get out of the way. I'll take it.

WARREN: My political corpse isn't even cold yet and you're taking my seat. No funeral, no eulogies?

CECE: No time for tears. Got to keep it moving, right Mr. Clayton?

WARREN: Right, CeCe. Keep it moving. I'm glad Laura saw something special in you.

CECE: You made her see it.

WARREN: And then another year passed. *(To CECE.)* How are your sons?

CECE: Doing great. Mr. Clayton: I got my GED. I'm up for a raise at my office. I'm making my sons proud. And I have another surprise coming: another baby. A daughter this time. We did it.

WARREN: No, you did that. That ain't my baby!! *(They laugh.)* But I'm happy for your CeCe.

CECE: I have my face again.

WARREN: I can see you. Or I will. Soon.

CECE: What do you mean?

WARREN: I was thinking about taking a little trip to sunny, beautiful… East Cleveland. What do you think?

WARREN takes out his suitcase.

CECE: You're going to visit East Cleveland? Voluntarily? You feeling okay, Warren?

WARREN: What? You don't want me to visit?

CECE: You must really have some good memories of this place.

WARREN: I have a few.

CECE: Well I can pick you up at the airport. And I sent you a book of poems. You can read them on the plane.

WARREN: Poems? I'm glad to see I've rubbed off on you.

CECE: Laura told me that you liked this guy so I went out and bought his book. I like one of his poems in particular. I read it to my daughter every night and I know that she can hear me.

WARREN: She sent me my favorite poet: Hafiz.

WARREN packs his suitcase as he speaks. He's making the trip back to East Cleveland through this poem.

CECE: "Fear is the cheapest room in the house.
    And I would like to see you living in better conditions.
    For your mother and my mother were friends.

WARREN: "I know the innkeeper in this part of the Universe
    Get some rest tonight
    Come to my verse tomorrow.
    We'll go speak to the Friend together

CECE: "I should not make any promise right now
    But I know if you pray,
    Somewhere in this world –
    something good will happen.

WARREN: "God wants to see
    More love and playfulness in your eyes
    For that is your greatest witness to Him.

CECE: "Your soul and my soul
    Once sat together in the Beloved's womb
    Playing footsie.

WARREN: "Your heart and my heart
    Are very, very old...

WARREN/CECE: Friends."

WARREN: Dear volunteers, East Cleveland is a rust-belt desert.
It is an America lacking access to banks, fully-stocked
grocery stores, and decent schools. It is a place that lost its
golden touch generations ago. It's all that follows me all
these years later. That even here, change is possible. And
during those long days and nights, amidst the cold and
darkness, and despite all my doubts, I saw the proof.

*SAM, BARBARA, and everyone else re-appears. They walk up to
WARREN. All look up at the fading lights.*

THE END

WWW.OBERONBOOKS.COM